GOVERNORS STATE UNIVERSI, ⟨ **Y0-CAS-292**
UNIVERSITY PARK
IL 60466

Using Test Data for Student Achievement

Answers to "No Child Left Behind"

Nancy W. Sindelar

Rowman & Littlefield Education
Lanham, Maryland • Toronto • Oxford
2006

Published in the United States of America
by Rowman & Littlefield Education
A Division of Rowman & Littlefield Publishers, Inc.
A wholly owned subsidiary of The Rowman & Littlefield Publishing Group, Inc.
4501 Forbes Boulevard, Suite 200, Lanham, Maryland 20706
www.rowmaneducation.com

PO Box 317
Oxford
OX2 9RU, UK

LB
3051
.S523
2006

Copyright © 2006 by Nancy W. Sindelar

All rights reserved. No part of this publication may be reproduced,
stored in a retrieval system, or transmitted in any form or by any
means, electronic, mechanical, photocopying, recording, or otherwise,
without the prior permission of the publisher.

British Library Cataloguing in Publication Information Available

Library of Congress Cataloging-in-Publication Data

Sindelar, Nancy W., 1944–
    Using test data for student achievement : answers to "no child left behind" /
Nancy W. Sindelar.
        p. cm.
    Includes bibliographical references and index.
    ISBN-13: 978-1-57886-369-3 (hardcover : alk. paper)
    ISBN-13: 978-1-57886-359-4 (pbk. : alk. paper)
    ISBN-10: 1-57886-369-4 (hardcover : alk. paper)
    ISBN-10: 1-57886-359-7 (pbk. : alk. paper)
    1. Educational tests and measurements—United States. 2. Educational
statistics—United States. 3. Academic achievement—United States.
4. Educational accountability—United States. 5. School improvement
programs—United States. I. Title.
LB3051.S523 2006
379.1'58—dc22   2005026946

∞™ The paper used in this publication meets the minimum requirements of
American National Standard for Information Sciences—Permanence of
Paper for Printed Library Materials, ANSI/NISO Z39.48-1992.
Manufactured in the United States of America.

To teach is to touch a life forever. . . .

Contents

Foreword

Never before have teachers been under so much pressure to raise student test scores. Greater demands for accountability in the form of higher test scores have come from many state education reforms over the past decade and most recently—and forcefully—from the federal government in the No Child Left Behind Act.

Many teachers, though, do not believe that an approach to school reform which mandates increases in test scores is the best way to bring about improvement in education. Although teachers and other educators have made known their frustrations, the policy makers are not relenting. For various reasons, the forces demanding increases in student test scores will have a potent impact on the schools for many years to come.

What are teachers to do? I suggest they make lemonade out of what they consider to be a lemon.

The pressure to raise test scores has revealed serious weaknesses in American education. What is taught is not always what is tested. Professional development is frequently not supportive of improvements in classroom teaching. The data from tests is often not used to analyze the needs of students or change teaching.

Today, educators—teachers, building principals, and district superintendents—have an opportunity to bring about significant changes to address these weaknesses, precisely because of the demands for greater accountability based on higher test scores. This book offers practical advice on how to make more sense out of American schooling. Nancy Sindelar draws on her experience as teacher and administrator to lay out a plan to improve student achievement by building a data-driven instructional system, aligning curriculum and assessments to standards, and using tests for instructional purposes and not just external accountability.

Educators are the ones who know schools best, but others, principally elected officials and business leaders, are setting the agenda for school reform. Educators ought to become more aggressive in identifying the ways that schools can do better in educating children. A good place to start is by mounting efforts to align curriculum, testing, and professional development, and to use test data to track student progress. These are all sound approaches for school improvement based on what happens in a school building and in a classroom.

Jack Jennings, president
Center on Education Policy

Acknowledgments

The ideas in this book were gathered over a lifetime of teaching and learning and a long career during which I had the opportunity and pleasure to work with many dedicated and thoughtful teachers and administrators. I especially wish to acknowledge the DuPage High School District 88 Board of Education, administration, teachers and staff. Through their support of technology and their collective dedication to student learning, a curriculum and assessment process was developed to help all students learn and reach their potential. I also want to thank Tom Koerner for his encouragement and guidance in the publication of this book and for truly being my lifelong teacher. Finally, my gratitude goes to my family for their support and interest as I attempt yet another journey into untraveled territory.

N. W. S.

Introduction

National and state educational reform efforts have focused on establishing higher academic standards and testing students to determine whether or not students are reaching the standards. The No Child Left Behind Act, signed in 2002, requires that all students meet state standards by 2014 and places schools into corrective action if they do not make adequate yearly progress toward the 2014 goal. Unfortunately, large numbers of students across the country are not reaching the standards, and reform efforts have not provided educators with a practical course of action to address the problem of students not meeting national and state standards.

State test results frequently are used to select and sort both individual students and schools into categories, labeled as "exceeding," "meeting," and "below" standards. Students who fail to meet standards may rationalize that they are not good at taking tests or do not care. Schools that do not meet standards may rationalize that students do not take the tests seriously or are too mobile or transient for schooling to make a difference.

However, when the national and state test scores and the percentages of students not meeting the standards appear in newspapers, cries of concern regarding student failure are heard from local citizens, parents, teachers, and school policy makers. While the answer to these cries of concern has been for states to continue to set standards and test to see if students are reaching them, testing alone does not increase student achievement. Increased achievement is based on solid instruction, a local curriculum and assessment system that is aligned with standards, and the use of local, state, and national assessment data to remediate students' weaknesses and build on their strengths.

While national and state assessments have produced an abundance of data regarding the strengths and weaknesses of students, little has been written to guide educators regarding the use of these data to increase student achievement. The purpose of *Using Test Data for Student Achievement: Answers to "No Child Left Behind"* is to provide elementary, middle school, and high school educators a step-by-step process guide for using test data to increase student achievement.

This book shows readers how to align a school's local curriculum and assessments to state and/or national standards, how to gather meaningful and useful student test data, how to interpret and use these data to revise curriculum and instructional practices, and how to provide the necessary interventions to help students succeed at meeting standards, the primary requirement of the No Child Left Behind Act. *Using Test Data for Student Achievement: Answers to "No Child Left Behind"* is a practical guide based on current research results and the author's professional experience.

CHAPTER 1

Why Schools Need to Use Data

There are two reasons schools need to use data: to address national, state, and local accountability issues and to increase the achievement of all students.

ACCOUNTABILITY

School boards, parents, communities, and politicians demand accountability of student learning. As a result, state and national standards have been established, and assessment data are being used to determine how much students have learned, whether standards have been met, and if teachers and administrators are doing the job they were hired to do. This practice constitutes using data for the sake of accountability.

The No Child Left Behind Act (NCLB), signed in January 2002, requires states to implement statewide accountability systems based on challenging state standards, regular testing of all students in grades 3–12 to determine the percentages of students reaching the standards, and annual statewide progress objectives ensuring that all groups of students reach proficiency by the year 2014. NCLB requires by 2005–2006 the creation of annual assessments in each state that measure what children know in reading and math. By 2007–2008 students also will be tested in science. Performance data from the required statewide tests must be disaggregated according to race, gender, ethnicity, English proficiency, migrant status, disability status, and low-income status, not only to demonstrate how well students are achieving overall, but also to show the state's and school's progress in closing the achievement gap between disadvantaged students and other groups of students.

Because achievement data must be disaggregated for subgroups, low-achieving subgroups can no longer be hidden in high-achieving districts (figure 1.1). Thus a school previously viewed as high achieving now faces the challenge of helping all students achieve or being viewed as failing under the new regulations.

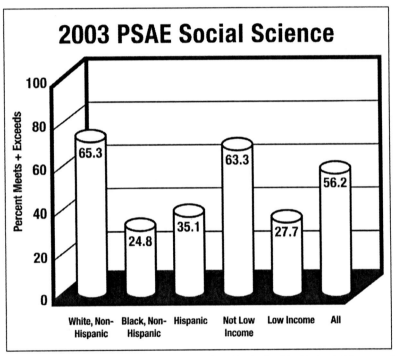

Figure 1.1.   Disaggregated Test Scores for Illinois Prairie State Achievement Exam (PSAE) in Social Science

This graph shows the various achievement levels for subgroups for the state of Illinois in social studies. Individual Illinois schools receive similar reports. Prior to NCLB, schools could report to communities the average score of all students, and low-achieving subgroups could be hidden in the average score. NCLB requires all subgroups to make adequate yearly progress toward the 2014 goal of meeting standards. Source: Adapted from Illinois State Board of Education, 2003, *PSAE Social Science*, www.isbe.net/assessment/PDF/PSAE2003data.pdf (accessed March 2005).

A school that fails to raise test scores for all groups faces major restructuring if the problem persists after five years; governance of a failing school could be converted to a charter school, turned over to a private management company, or taken over by the state. After two years of failure, children in a chronically failing school are given the chance to choose a different public school and after three years of failure the right to use some of their school's Title I funding to purchase tutoring from a state-approved private company selected by the students or their parents (Jennings, Rentner, and Kober 2002, 2).

According to the U.S. Department of Education, the purpose of NCLB is to "empower parents, citizens, educators, administrators, and policymakers with data from . . . annual assessments [and] give parents information about the quality of their children's schools, the qualifications of teachers, and their children's progress in key subjects" (U.S. Department of Education 2002b, 1).

NCLB requires school districts to publish annual report cards indicating student achievement for the district and for each school. NCLB is linked with federal funding, school choice, and accountability measures that create a charge for teachers and administrators to become skilled at using data to meet the accountability demands of this legislation. School districts that do not demonstrate adequate yearly progress (AYP) are "subject to improvement, corrective action, and restructuring measures aimed at getting them back on course to meet state standards" (U.S. Department of Education 2002a, 1).

Public access to student achievement data presents a new accountability challenge for many schools. However, it also creates an opportunity for school districts to dialogue with parents and community members about the teaching, learning, and assessment process and engage community members in answering the important curriculum question, What should students know and be able to do? Though there continue to be changes in the details of implementing NCLB, it is not likely that the call for accountability based on aligned standards, assessments, and accountability systems will go away. (See rule changes in NCLB in Key Resources at the end of the chapter.) Fifty states have established or are in the process of establishing academic standards, and schools realize that state standards are not a passing fad because they are now embedded in state tests with test results reported to the public.

ACHIEVEMENT

Though federal and state laws have required the use of data for accountability in closing the achievement gap, an even greater argument for using data is to increase student achievement at *all levels in all schools*. The phrase "closing the achievement gap" has the negative implication that students at the top cannot get any better. Yet research argues that the consistent use of data is key to helping all students, including those at the top, improve.

Richard Stiggins (2002) makes the important distinction between "assessment of learning" for accountability purposes and "assessment for learning" for student achievement purposes (30). Assessments of learning provide evidence of student achievement for public reporting and accountability. Assessments for learning help students learn because they identify a student's strengths and weaknesses and provide information so that the teacher can remediate the student's weaknesses and build on the strengths. At this point, state tests are being used primarily as assessments of learning. They determine which schools and which students "exceed," "meet," and fall "below" state standards (figure 1.2). For the purposes of NCLB, they document which schools have met AYP, and in what subjects.

Educational research has long advocated assessment for learning by using test data to identify students' strengths and weaknesses in order to aid teaching and learning and increase student achievement. In the early 1980s the effective schools research revealed that successful schools frequently monitored students' progress. Ron Edmonds (as cited in Bullard and Taylor 1993, 17) advocated the use of data when he pronounced that in effective schools "feedback on

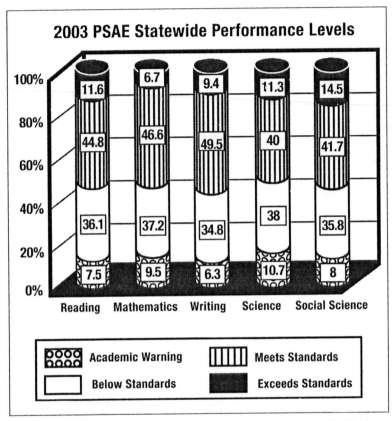

2003 PSAE Statewide Performance Levels

Figure 1.2.   2003 State of Illinois Performance Levels on the Prairie State Achievement Exam

Illinois students are divided into four categories based on their performance on the state test. Both schools and individual students receive similar reports regarding their ability to meet the Illinois learning standards.

Source: Adapted from Illinois State Board of Education, *2003 Statewide Performance Levels,* www.isbe.net/assessment/PDF/PSAE2003data.pdf (accessed March 2005).

student progress is frequently obtained [and] the results of testing are used to improve individual student performance and also to improve the instructional program."

Carl Glickman (1993) urged educators to seek clear indicators by asking, "What data or information about effectiveness are currently collected?" "How complete are the data?" "How does the school community share the data and use them for setting priorities and determining actions?" Glickman (1993) advocated setting achievement-oriented goals, stating that "the litmus test for a good school [was] the solid, purposeful, enduring results it tries to obtain for its students" (50–51). More recently, Michael Fullan (2001) urged schools to work toward assessment literacy by examining student performance data, creating capacity to examine student data and make sense of them, disaggregating data to identify subgroups that may be disadvantaged or underperforming, and, based on data, making changes in teaching and action plans (14).

Though modern assessment software has made it easier for schools to score, analyze, and store student test data, educators have had access to the data for years. However, Rosenholtz (1991) found that "despite school's espoused goals of student learning . . . principals rarely use data on student achievement to . . . monitor students' performance, even though such data are frequently available" (16).

The failure to use data to increase student achievement is rooted in the fact that few states require knowledge of assessment for either teacher or administrator certification, and few universities include courses in assessment in their teacher and administrator training programs. As a result, state test scores are reported to the public in newspaper headlines, but little is done with the data to improve teaching and student learning.

It is not unusual for teachers to not "own" the data from state tests because they do not believe the state has tested the true learning that has taken place in their classrooms. Teachers frequently criticize state tests because they do not test what is being taught. In many schools, teachers and administrators do not see much relationship between what is being taught and assessed at the local or school level and the state standards, which are assessed by state tests required by NCLB.

For students to learn and for students to meet or exceed state standards, schools must develop a relationship between the local curriculum, instructional and assessment practices, and the state standards.

Using data from state tests to simply select and sort schools and students by state test scores is not going to increase student achievement. State test data must be used to identify strengths and weaknesses in curriculum, assessment, and students' knowledge before an increase in learning and achievement can take place. If schools would align their local curriculum and assessments to state and national standards, then everyday teaching and learning experiences would lead to higher achievement on state tests. While this practice may seem logical, it is not taking place in most schools across the country.

It is not unusual for lessons to be taught in isolation from state standards. Some districts believe in hiring the best teachers and then staying out of their way. In many schools, teachers develop their own curriculum and assessments, which may or may not be linked to national or state standards. Also, curriculum for a particular course or grade may be tied to a textbook that may not address a particular standard.

In Illinois, for example, students are tested on their knowledge of economics at the end of eleventh grade. The learning standards expect eleventh-grade high school students to know all of the following:

A. Understand how different economic systems operate in the exchange, production, and distribution and consumption of goods and services.

15.A.5a Explain the impact of various determinants of economic growth (e.g., investments in human/physical capital, research and development, technological change) on the economy.

15.A.5b Analyze the impact of economic growth.

15.A.5c Analyze the impact of various determinants on the levels of GDP (e.g., quantity/quality of natural/capital resources, size/skills of the labor force).

15.A.5d Explain the comparative value of the Consumer Price Index (e.g., goods and services in one year with earlier or later periods).

B. Understand that scarcity necessitates choices by consumers.

15.B.1 Explain why consumers must make choices.

15.B.2a Identify factors that affect how consumers make their choices.

15.B.2b Explain the relationship between the quantity of goods/services purchased and their price.

15.B.2c Explain that when a choice is made, something else is given up.

15.B.3a Describe the "market clearing price" of a good or service.

15.B.3b Explain the effects of choice and competition on individuals and the economy as a whole.

15.B.4a Explain the costs and benefits of making consumer purchases through differing means (e.g., credit, cash).

15.B.4b Analyze the impact of current events (e.g., weather/natural disasters, wars) on consumer prices.

15.B.5a Analyze the impact of changes in non-price determinants (e.g., changes in consumer income, changes in tastes and preferences) on consumer demand.

15.B.5b Analyze how inflation and interest rates affect consumer purchasing power.

15.B.5c Analyze elasticity as it applies to supply and demand and consumer decisions.

C. Understand that scarcity necessitates choices by producers.

15.C.1a Describe how human, natural, and capital resources are used to produce goods and services.

15.C.1b Identify limitations in resources that force producers to make choices about what to produce.

15.C.2a Describe the relationship between price and quantity supplied of a good or service.

15.C.2b Identify and explain examples of competition in the economy.

15.C.2c Describe how entrepreneurs take risks in order to produce goods or services.

15.C.3 Identify and explain the effects of various incentives to produce a good or service.

15.C.4a Analyze the impact of political actions and natural phenomena (e.g., wars, legislation, natural disaster) on producers and production decisions.

15.C.4b Explain the importance of research, development, invention, technology, and entrepreneurship to the United States economy.

15.C.5a Explain how competition is maintained in the United States economy and how the level of competition varies in differing market structures (e.g., monopoly, oligopoly, monopolistic and perfect competition).

15.C.5b Explain how changes in non-price determinants of supply (e.g., number of producers) affect producer decisions.

15.C.5c Explain how government intervention with market prices can cause shortages or surpluses of a good or service (e.g., minimum wage policies, rent freezes, farm subsidies).

D. Understand trade as an exchange of goods or services.

15.D.1a Demonstrate the benefits of simple voluntary exchanges.

15.D.1b Know that barter is a type of exchange and that money makes exchange easier.

15.D.2a Explain why people and countries voluntarily exchange goods and services.

15.D.2b Describe the relationships among specialization, division of labor, productivity of workers and interdependence among producers and consumers.

15.D.3a Explain the effects of increasing and declining imports and exports to an individual and to the nation's economy as a whole.

15.D.3b Explain how comparative advantage forms the basis for specialization and trade among nations.

15.D.3c Explain how workers can affect their productivity through training and by using tools, machinery and technology.

15.D.4a Explain the meaning and importance of "balance of trade" and how trade surpluses and deficits between nations are determined.

15.D.4b Describe the relationships between the availability and price of a nation's resources and its comparative advantage in relation to other nations.

15.D.4c Describe the impact of worker productivity (output per worker) on business, the worker, and the consumer.

15.D.5a Explain how transaction costs affect decisions to produce or consume.

15.D.5b Analyze why trade barriers and exchange rates affect the flow of goods and services among nations.

15.D.5c Explain how technology has affected trade in the areas of transportation, communication, finance, and manufacturing.

E. Understand the impact of government policies and decisions on production and consumption in the economy.

15.E.1 Identify goods and services provided by government.

15E.2a Explain how and why public goods and services are provided.

15.E.2b Identify which public goods and services are provided by differing levels of government.

15.E.3a Identify the types of taxes levied by differing levels of governments (e.g., income tax, sales tax, property tax).

15.E.3b Explain how laws and government policies (e.g., property rights, contract enforcement, standard weights/measurements) establish rules that help a market economy function effectively.

15.E.4a Explain why government may intervene in a market economy.

15.E.4b Describe social and environmental benefits and consequences of production and consumption.

15.E.4c Analyze the relationship between a country's science/technology policies and its level and balance of trade.

15.E.5a Explain how and why government redistributes income in the economy.

15.E.5b Describe how fiscal, monetary, and regulatory policies affect overall levels of employment, output, and consumption.

15.E.5c Describe key schools of thought (e.g., classical, Keynesian, monetarist, supply-side) and explain their impact on government policies. (Illinois State Board of Education 1997b, 46–49)

Yet most students study U.S. history in eleventh grade and receive little exposure to economics elsewhere in their studies. As a result, many eleventh-grade students do not meet the economic standards tested on the Illinois Prairie State Achievement Test because (1) economics is not included in their eleventh-grade curriculum, (2) it is not included in their textbook, (3) supplementary material on economics has not been provided or taught to them, and/or (4) they have not studied economics previously.

Schools need to build a common local curriculum and assessment program that is tied to standards and monitor local test data to see whether or not students are learning the standards-based material that is being taught. Currently, many schools fail to collect and analyze data to assess how well students are performing on the school's local curriculum. The systematic analysis of local test data, which is a form of assessment for learning, would show teachers and administrators what students know and what needs to be taught or retaught. If local curriculum and assessments are aligned with state standards, then local test data can be used to determine how well students are progressing toward learning the state standards and predict student performance on state tests before the tests are even given. Many schools are failing to meet NCLB requirements because local curriculum and assessments and local instruction are totally divorced from state standards.

For many schools, the process of aligning the local curriculum and assessments with state standards will simply mean auditing the local curriculum against the state standards and making minor adjustments. For other schools, aligning local curriculum and assessments with state standards will first require defining what the local curriculum really is. This will require collecting local teaching units and tests to build a common curriculum and assessment program.

While this process will take time and effort, it does not cost a lot of money and can easily be accomplished by a committed school leader and grade/subject teacher teams who agree to meet on a regular basis to align their local curriculum and assessments to state standards, monitor local test results for students' strengths and weaknesses, and develop interventions to remediate deficiencies in the areas in which students are weak. This process does not require extensive knowledge of curriculum construction, assessment design, or statistics. It merely requires a genuine commitment to helping all students achieve at a higher level.

KEY RESOURCES

Rule Changes in NCLB

Given the number of requirements placed on schools by the NCLB legislation and the severity of consequences for schools not meeting the various requirements, it is not surprising that there have been numerous requests for and changes in the guidelines for implementing NCLB.

In 2004 alone, forty-seven states asked the U.S. Department of Education to approve changes to their NCLB accountability plans. In many cases these changes have made it easier for schools and districts to show adequately yearly progress. By accessing the Center on Education Policy website (www.cep-dc.org), schools can learn about recent changes that will impact the implementation of NCLB in their state and for their school. Access the link to "Rule Changes Could Help More Schools Meet Test Score Targets for the No Child Left Behind Act," October 22, 2004.

CHAPTER 2

Building a Data-Driven Instructional System at the School or District Level

Much has been written about the pros and cons of testing. The public and the government want accountability, and parents and school communities search for objective proof of student achievement. Yet some teachers argue that testing takes away from valuable instructional time and thus negatively affects achievement. However, almost everyone wants to know if students are achieving at a higher level than they did in the past, as well as how their local school compares with schools across the state, country, and world. Testing seems to be a common solution to answering questions about what students have learned.

Yet merely testing students' knowledge of state standards, as required by the No Child Left Behind Act, does not increase achievement or reform schools. It selects and sorts students and schools by telling us which students and which schools meet standards, exceed standards, and fail standards. Like the final score at the end of a football game, testing alone does not tell us anything about how the game was played. It merely tells us who won or lost.

Rather, it is the combination of assessments of learning (such as state tests) and assessments for learning (such as local assessments aligned to a standards-based curriculum) and the consistent use of test data from both forms of tests that allows schools to not only become more accountable for student learning but also increase student achievement. Consistent use of test data provides educators with valuable information regarding the strengths and weaknesses of students, the curriculum, and instructional practices and materials.

If a new teaching strategy is used or a textbook is changed, reliable test data will indicate if these changes contributed to increased

13

achievement. The data from local assessments for learning will immediately show teachers and administrators if the change affected learning positively and thus led to higher scores on the high-stakes state test, which is an assessment of learning.

THE THREE BASIC QUESTIONS

While using local assessment data is a key component in raising student achievement, a system for gathering and using data first needs to be developed and three basic questions need to be asked and answered before data can be gathered and used effectively.

First, schools need to ask, *What do students need to know and be able to do?* While the first question is answered in most, if not all, states by state standards, schools also should seek input from the larger school community and ask groups of parents, teachers, students, and community members, What do students need to know and what should they be able to do to be successful in the twenty-first century? Though most school communities want students to meet or exceed standards on the state tests, they will have additional priorities they believe are important for their children.

A community's educational priorities will be heartfelt and varied, and to some extent based on the geographic area and socioeconomic level of the community. When a parent-community group located along Chicago's suburban high-tech corridor was asked this basic curriculum question, the response basically fell into three categories. All students need superior skills in math, writing, and science. All students need to be technologically literate. All students need greater sensitivity to and understanding of a multicultural society. While many school communities would agree with these three findings, the answer to the question, What do we want students to know and be able to do? varies from state to state and from community to community. Thus the first step in the process of using data to increase student achievement is to ask the question, What do students need to know and be able to do to be successful in the twenty-first century?

and then distill the feedback into an answer for a specific school or district.

Unfortunately, many schools never get beyond asking and answering this question. The answer invariably sounds like a mission statement about students needing to possess the necessary skills to become lifelong learners and caring members of the community, and nothing changes. The trick is to transform the answer into a local curriculum that reflects local values and state and national standards and that can be taught and measured.

Because the school community mentioned earlier valued computer literacy both as a means for accessing academic information and as a necessary workplace skill, a computer literacy graduation requirement was added, and the existing curriculum was infused with state-of-the-art hardware and software to enhance students' computer literacy skills in each discipline. Because of the importance of computer literacy throughout the curriculum, students were required to demonstrate their computer literacy skill freshman year or else enroll in a required computer literacy class sophomore year.

The school community also wanted to see improvement in state test scores in the areas of math and science and increased the graduation requirement in science from one year to two years and required that the existing two-year math requirement include courses in algebra and geometry. General math, which previously had met the math requirement, became an elective and no longer fulfilled one year of the two-year math requirement because it did not sufficiently address algebra and geometry, which was assessed on the state test.

Graduation requirements were aligned with the state standards, math and science requirements were increased, and a computer literacy requirement was added. The graduation requirements were then defined by specific courses meeting the requirements. Existing courses were aligned to graduation requirements, and new courses were added where there were gaps. Similarly, courses such as general math that no longer specifically met requirements became electives or were dropped.

Man in Harmony with Nature, an English course introduced in the 1960s that advanced students' understanding of literature and man's relationship to his environment, was dropped because it did not address the Illinois learning standards, which emphasize American literature, literary conventions and devices, speech, and writing. After much debate, Man in Harmony with Nature was dropped, and students were required to fulfill their graduation requirements in English with courses that were more closely tied to the Illinois learning standards.

After all courses were aligned to the new graduation requirements and the state learning standards, specific, measurable common course objectives were developed for each course and also were aligned with the state learning standards. These common course objectives were developed by teacher teams, and all sections of a grade level or course followed them. When course objectives were limited to eight to ten per semester, course material that was not tied to the Illinois learning standards was eliminated from the curriculum.

This process tightened curriculum to address the newly defined graduation requirements and the state standards. Because course material that was not aligned with the Illinois learning standards was eliminated, there was room in the curriculum to add new course objectives for areas and state standards that were not being addressed by the old curriculum.

After schools answer the first question, What do students need to know and be able to do? and adjust their curricula accordingly, the next step in the process is to answer a second question: *How will we know if students have learned it and can do it?* Schools and districts can answer this question by devising a common local assessment for each course or grade level. Local assessment questions should be tied to the course objectives and state standards, and an item analysis of local assessment answers completed after each exam. The item analysis by objective will tell teachers and administrators what students are learning, what they are not learning, and, in some cases, indicate that the test contains poorly written test questions that are confusing or misleading to students and need to be rewritten.

After each common local assessment is administered to students, teachers need to meet in subject area teams to review the exam results for their class individually as well as the results for all students taking the common local assessment. Teachers immediately will see what their students know and what they don't know, and powerful, soul-searching discussions will ensue regarding curriculum, instructional methods, pacing, and more.

The teacher team discussions that result from answering the second question, How will we know if students have learned it and can do it? will lead to the first step in answering the third question and also initiate the process of using data from local assessments for learning to increase student achievement.

The third question schools need to answer is, *What will we do if students don't know it and can't do it?* Schools and districts can use student test data to answer the third question in at least three ways:

1. Use data to change the curriculum. Schools will find that item analysis of local assessment exam questions will reveal strengths and weaknesses in the curriculum. For example, the school previously mentioned learned that students in entry-level math classes were weak in mathematical measurement. They didn't know it and they couldn't do it. The results of local common exams were reflected by state test scores.

As a result of local and state test data, the school changed textbooks, purchased and used rulers, tape measures, and other measuring devices, and allocated more time in the curriculum to the study of measurement. A year later, students' test scores on both local and state assessments showed their understanding of and ability to use measurement had improved.

2. Use data to refocus and improve instruction. While the measurement example revealed a weakness in the curriculum, item analysis by objective also will reveal the strengths and weaknesses of individual teachers. One teacher's students may score high on the causes of the Civil War while another's may score in a much lower range. The local assessment data and time for teacher team meetings will stimulate teachers to examine and share their teaching strategies, materials, and pacing and will provide a powerful internal resource for improving instruction.

The common local assessments will not signal to teachers that the unit of instruction is over and it's time to move on. Rather, the item analysis of the common local assessments and time for teacher team meetings to discuss local assessment results will create an opportunity for professional reflection and dialogue about teaching strategies and ways to improve student achievement.

3. Use data to remediate individual student weaknesses and build on individual strengths. With this curriculum and assessment model in place, schools and districts will have an abundance of data regarding students' individual strengths and weaknesses. This information can be used to increase individual student achievement by placing students in the most appropriate courses and to recommend individual summer programs and tutoring opportunities to increase student achievement by remediating individual weaknesses. A student who reads two or more years below grade level should be required to take a reading class to improve reading skills. Schools should not pass students along to the next grade level if they lack the required skills to succeed in the course. Rather, the interventions described here and those discussed in chapter 6 should be used to help students reach the appropriate achievement level before they are moved to the next grade level.

Schools that align their local curriculum and assessments to standards and then use local student test data to make changes in curriculum and instructional practices and provide strategic interventions to remediate student weaknesses will increase student achievement. These examples illustrate how assessments for learning can be developed and used to make changes in instruction. Because data from common local assessments for learning can be immediately available to teachers and administrators, important changes can be made and validated before high-stakes assessments of learning take place.

Any school or district, regardless of size or operating budget, can easily replicate this process of developing a data-driven instructional system, and the chapters that follow provide specific guidelines and materials. Though the process is not expensive, it is not a quick fix. It takes time, hard work, and consistent leadership.

GETTING TEACHERS TO BUY IN

Unfortunately, the process of developing common curriculum and assessments and using the data from these efforts is often challenged by teachers. Common curriculum is viewed as a threat to academic freedom and creativity, and common assessments yield objective data and a level of accountability that reveal teacher effectiveness.

Yet, even given these concerns, it is still possible to persuade teachers to buy in and use data to drive student achievement. It is helpful to begin the "buy-in" process to develop common curriculum by beginning with the subject areas that are most closely aligned to the state standards and have the fewest differences in teachers' individually developed curricula. Math and modern languages usually fall into this category because of the vertical sequencing inherently required by these disciplines.

After areas for common curriculum are identified, teachers should be organized into grade level or subject area teams to create common course objectives. Teachers will learn in their team meetings that their individual curricula are more similar than they thought and will see the gaps between their taught curricula and the state standards. After a few meetings teachers will be able to agree on common objectives and write new objectives for standards that were not addressed by the old curriculum.

It will become obvious to teacher teams that additional materials should be selected to engage students in learning the new objectives.

Once teachers are organized into curriculum teams and given time to meet, agreement regarding a common curriculum will be reached, and common course objectives will become a reality. This process can be repeated in each subject area until an entire district or school has a common curriculum.

Common assessments can then be created by using individual teacher tests and linking the best test items to access the new common course objectives. This process will reveal that there are more similarities than differences in teachers' individual test items. However, teachers will be quick choose the "best" items for the new common local assessment and write new test items for the new curriculum objectives, which previously had not been tested.

Once the teachers have begun the process working together to build common curriculum and assessments, the buy in to use data to drive student achievement begins. Teachers find that working with colleagues on courses they will be teaching is a powerful form of staff development. They build on one another's strengths by sharing methods, ideas, and materials to improve their teaching and their students' learning. When the data from the common assessments are available, teachers are able to see the fruits of their labors: the individual strengths and weaknesses of their students.

Assessment data gives teachers objective information about what students have learned and begins the important discussion regarding the question, What will we do if they don't know it? More frequently than not, the answers to these questions are obvious. Spend more time on a topic, change the textbook, or use a different teaching method. Because the data are so meaningful in increasing student achievement, teachers buy into the process, and data-driven instruction becomes an important part of the school culture.

AUTHOR'S NOTE

The examples shared in this chapter were the result of a curriculum and assessment process that took place at DuPage High School

District 88, where the author was assistant superintendent for curriculum, instruction, and assessment.

The three basic questions, What should students know and be able to do? How will we know if students know it? and What will we do if they don't know it? were derived from a clinical observation preconference form developed for use by DuPage High School District 88 by Bellon and Associates in 1987 (see figure 7.1). Similar questions are posed by Richard DuFour, Rebecca DuFour, Robert Eaker, and Gayle Karhanek (2004) in *Whatever It Takes: How Professional Learning Communities Respond When Kids Don't Learn.*

CHAPTER 3

Aligning Curriculum
and Assessments with Standards

ALIGNING CURRICULUM WITH STANDARDS

A school's curriculum is a document that answers the question, What do you want students to know and be able to do? Whether it is tied to state standards, national standards, or locally developed standards, the curriculum tells teachers, students, parents, and administrators what is to be taught and what is not to be taught.

Unfortunately, in many schools the curriculum is a dusty book or collection of papers that is placed on a shelf and forgotten. However well written and well intentioned, sometimes it is not followed by classroom teachers, not aligned with local assessments, and/or not aligned to state or national standards. Schools with curriculum in this status should not feel guilty. They are not alone. However, schools that want to build a data-driven instructional program first must build a living, usable common curriculum that is used and updated by teachers and aligned to state or national standards. They can achieve this by following the five steps described below for building and updating a common curriculum.

1. Document what is being taught by collecting materials and information to develop common curriculum objectives that determine what currently is being taught at each grade level in each subject area. Grade level/subject area teacher teams work well for this process. Teacher teams can describe the existing curricula by collecting unit plans, syllabi, and major projects. From this information, common curriculum/course objectives for the grade and subject can be defined or revised by the teams. Teachers decide the curriculum they all will follow and the pacing they all will use.

Common curriculum pacing means that teachers agree to cover the same material at a similar rate (e.g., chapters 1–8 will be taught by Thanksgiving). Developing a common curriculum and agreeing on pacing are key to developing a system for collecting data because it is at this step teachers document what students should know, when they should know it, and at a key juncture, assess students to determine if they know it.

Teachers may initially feel threatened by the idea of developing a common curriculum. For example, some English teachers have opposed following a common curriculum and giving a common exam, believing such standardization stifles their creativity as teachers and inhibits them from teaching their favorite novels and short stories. They have been known to view the common curriculum as "Procrustean," after the mythological character who required his visitors to be the same size to fit his bed and either stretched them or cut off their legs.

However, after the initial team meeting, most teachers thoroughly enjoy getting together with their colleagues to discuss what they are teaching in their classrooms and what is working. Teacher team meetings to discuss what students should know and when they should learn it lead to an improved curriculum and to more thoughtful teaching and learning. Generally, when teachers meet in grade level and/or subject area teams and compare what they are teaching, they find very few differences in the course of study they each individually designed, are fascinated by the array of methods and materials their colleagues use to engage students with the subject matter, and soon decide to "share the wealth" within their grade-level teams on a regular basis.

Similarly, when teachers compare their individually developed final exams, they are impressed by their colleagues' creativity and "borrow" the best test items from one another to build the new common exam. In the initial team meetings, as teachers learn they have much to share with and learn from their colleagues, they take a major step toward developing a common curriculum and a common final assessment.

2. Compare common curriculum objectives with state/national standards. Once course objectives have been developed for a given grade level and subject area, the next step is to compare what is being taught with what should be taught, what is being learned with what should be learned. If students are going to do well on state and national exams, then the topics on those exams must be taught and locally assessed at the appropriate grade level. This seems like common sense. Yet in working with schools, I have found that key topics on state tests are not taught at all or are not taught at the appropriate grade level. A frequent cause for this situation is that a topic on the state test is not in the course textbook. As one Illinois principal recently said, "It's no wonder our students don't do well on this part of the state test. It's not covered in our textbook!"

In a number of states earth science is expected to be covered prior to eleventh grade and is tested on the state test. Yet it is often neglected in the curriculum. Often high schools have a two-year science requirement. All freshmen take biology; all sophomores take physical science; some juniors take physics; and some seniors take chemistry. Given this sequence of courses, it is not surprising that students do not do well on the earth science questions on the eleventh-grade state test.

The solution is not to add another course, but to see where the key earth science objectives can be added to the existing biology and physical science curricula. Once the biology and physical science teacher teams understand the challenge, they usually are quite adept at enhancing the existing curricula to include the key earth science objectives and assess these new objectives on the common, local assessments. As a result of these changes, students learn the state earth science objectives and the scores go up on the state test.

The second issue that arises when the taught curriculum is compared to state standards is that curricular redundancies appear. Schools often find that they are teaching and testing the same objective over and over. In many states American history is taught both at eighth grade and eleventh grade. Though eleventh-grade history covers the material in greater depth, this is one subject area that often contains unnecessary duplication. It is important to eliminate redundancies so that time to study new material can be found by eliminating a unit that has previously been covered and learned by students.

Many states require that students study and pass a test on state and federal constitutions in eighth grade and eleventh grade. The eleventh-grade Constitution test usually is in addition to the state's test of standards. While it may be a requirement for students to take a Constitution test in eleventh grade, most states to not specify when this test must be taken. Thus it is possible to create time for studying new subject material tested on the state test by moving the eleventh-grade study of the Constitution until after the state test of standards. Frequently, students' prior knowledge of the Constitution is adequate for doing well on the state's test of standards, and the thorough, in-depth eleventh-grade study of the Constitution can take place in a separate unit or project at the end of the school year and after the state's test of standards.

The third issue that arises is that of the "favorite unit" or lesson that does not contribute to any curricular goal or state standard or a unit that is overtaught because the teacher likes the subject. Sometimes it is difficult work to convince the Civil War expert to trim the unit to the stated objectives when he or she is used to spending the majority of the semester covering the Civil War in depth, while failing to cover other important topics. Though dropping material from an individual teacher's informal curriculum is challenging work, teacher teams are generally successful at convincing team members that any subject matter not contributing to the essential focus of the curriculum should be eliminated.

3. Revise the curriculum to eliminate redundancies and fill in gaps. When the current curriculum is compared to the standards, teacher teams can easily identify redundancies and gaps in what is being taught. What is often difficult is actually making the changes to align the curriculum to the standards. Two main arguments tend to emerge.

First, in schools where teachers have developed their own teaching units and have not been asked to follow a common curriculum, there may be resistance to change. At this point leaders need to be strong and foster a commitment to a common curriculum that is focused on standards. Though favorite units or projects may be eliminated or revised, teachers need to understand that a common, standards-based curriculum does not limit opportunities for creative teaching and approaches to subject matter. They also may need to be reminded that as state certified teachers, they are required to teach the school's agreed-on curriculum.

Second, at this point the idea of "teaching to the test" may be raised, with the implication that this is not good educational practice. The point to be made here is that the school is building a common curriculum that is tied to standards, and it is the students' knowledge of the standards that the state is testing.

Some teachers are opposed to the state telling them what to teach. Yet when teachers actually examine the standards, most agree that the standards are worthwhile, challenging topics that should be learned by students.

4. Link curriculum objectives to standards. Once the curriculum for a given grade and subject area is complete and the redundancies and gaps have been eliminated, the course objectives should be linked to the state standards. (See Key Resources at the end of this chapter.) This linkage is a check for ensuring that all standards are being covered and will be helpful as teachers develop and score the common, local assessments.

While several formats for curriculum and assessment alignment to standards are provided (see figures 3.1 and 3.2), schools are free to modify these formats or their existing formats to be teacher-friendly, user-friendly documents. (See Key Resources.) The elements that should exist in the curriculum formats are

- clearly stated curriculum objectives
- an assessment for each objective

- a notation regarding the state standard that the objective and the assessment address

School:_____

Grade/Subject: _____

Curriculum Objective and State Standard:_____

_____

Materials	Activities	Common Assessments

Figure 3.1.   Sample Curriculum Map. This map format should be reproduced for each standard taught at a particular grade level or course.

Course Title/Grade Level: _____

Course Code: _____

Course Objective (State Standard): _____

Materials Used: First Semester: _____

Second Semester: _____

Instructional Objective	Method of Evaluation

Figure 3.2.   Sample Course Outline/Curriculum Map. See tables 3.1 and 3.2 for additional clarification.

5. Examine horizontal and vertical alignment issues. The final touch to revising and refining the curriculum is to attend to horizontal and vertical alignment issues. *Horizontal alignment* means checking to see that all teachers at the same grade and subject area are following a common curriculum and moving through it at about the same pace. When all teachers at a given grade and subject level develop and follow a common curriculum that addresses standards and give at least some key common assessments, it becomes possible to collect uniform data to monitor students' progress in learning the standards.

As curriculum is developed at the same grades for other subjects, other horizontal issues will arise. For example, freshmen may be asked to draw graphs in biology before they are taught how to graph in algebra. This is a mistake in horizontal alignment. Students feel they are being asked to do something they don't understand by their biology teacher, and when it comes time for them to learn graphing in algebra, they have an attitude of "We did this already."

A few team meetings between biology and algebra teachers can correct the situation and make for more powerful teaching and learning. The graphing unit should be moved up in the algebra curriculum, so that it is appropriately taught by the math teachers, and the biology teachers then are able to show their students how graphing is an application of what students have learned in algebra, thus reinforcing and applying what students had learned previously.

Vertical alignment deals with sequence or what students have learned before and after a given grade level. Once curriculum has been developed for a given subject at a number of grade levels, it is a good idea to have vertical teacher team meetings to review course objectives for each grade level. Thus fifth-, sixth-, seventh-, and eighth-grade teachers would review the math curriculum to make certain that each grade level builds on previous levels and prepares students for what is to follow.

Vertical teams also look for vertical gaps and redundancies, again with standards in mind. For example, state standards may be met by teaching short stories to students in ninth-grade English classes and then again in tenth-grade English classes. By tenth grade the students may be tired of reading short stories. The result of vertical team meetings would be to make the curriculum more interesting and engaging to students by using a different genre to teach the tenth-grade course objectives.

COMMUNICATING STANDARDS AND EXPECTATIONS

The curriculum needs to be a living document that is used and revised. Teachers need to know and teach the course objectives, understand their relationship to state or national standards, and use the common assessments to measure what has been learned by their students. Once the curriculum has been written, it will be necessary to revise and update it to adjust for pacing needs, student learning needs, and the updating of materials.

Other school documents also should reflect the common curriculum. If a school has a standardized lesson plan format or plan book, it should have a clear place for course objectives that will be taught and a definite time for common assessments to be given. Similarly, teacher evaluations and observation forms are a good place to note and reinforce the curricular process. If a preobservation conference is used prior to the classroom observation, there should be discussion about the objectives of the lesson and the parts of the curriculum and the standards that will be addressed by the lesson. All the observer needs to ask is, What state standard is being addressed in today's lesson? Making the curriculum part of the lesson planning process and the teacher evaluation process is a means of reinforcing the point that the common, standards-based curriculum is an important part of the teaching and learning process, not a document that sits on a shelf and gathers dust.

When aligning curriculum and assessments to standards, teacher teams need to stay focused on the standard. Because most teachers are highly engaged with the content they teach, it is easy for them to lose focus and thus overteach one standard and forget another. It also is common for new topics to be added to the curriculum but never assessed. Teacher teams need to be disciplined about making both the curriculum and the assessments reflect the standards.

ALIGNING LOCAL ASSESSMENTS TO STANDARDS

Each curricular objective should be assessed, and data from assessments should be collected and reviewed by individual teachers and teacher teams on a regular basis. This practice answers the question, How will you know if students have learned what they need to know and be able to do? The options on assessment are many. What is important is for teacher teams decide on key common assessments and when they will be given. What follows are the steps for aligning assessments to a local, standards-based curriculum:

1. *Once standards-based curriculum objectives have been developed for each grade-level subject area or course, one or more methods of assessment should be identified for assessing each objective.* The assessment of an objective may be a portion of a test or a local assessment that tests students' understanding of a number of objectives. This assessment would look similar to the traditional unit test or final exam. However, it also could be a rubric-graded project or a lab exercise. In this case, the rubric would contain the criteria or the objectives that were taught to the students, and the teacher would grade the students based on their knowledge of each of the criteria or objectives. Either type of assessment would test students' understanding of the curriculum objective(s) and state standard.

2. *Teacher teams should consider developing a portion of the assessment that is similar in format to the state's method of assessment.* If students are familiar with the test format when they take the state test, they will perform better. Thus it is good practice to have at least a portion of the local, common assessment mirror the format of the high-stakes state or summative assessment. A number of schools model this practice by using the state's writing rubric for grading students' local written work, thus providing teacher and students

with a vocabulary about writing and scoring that is similar to the state's as well as identifying students' strengths and weaknesses in writing before the state writing assessment.

3. *When the type of assessment has been determined, the teacher team should agree on the test items or the criteria for the project and the associated common rubric.* If the curriculum is aligned with standards and test items are aligned with the curriculum, the assessment will be aligned with standards. However, whether using a pin file or another form of notation, test items should also be linked to individual curriculum objectives.

Table 3.1 is taken from a high school–level curriculum and assessment map outlining the objectives and assessments for studying the scientific method in a high school biology class. The notation in parentheses references the state standards in science.

The teacher team that developed the biology example (table 3.1) made the following decisions:

1. All freshmen took biology, and it was important that students understood the scientific method, for success in biology and future science classes and because it was a key standard (table 3.2) assessed by the state PSAE exam.
2. Applying the scientific method was important enough to be a course objective for biology.
3. As a course objective, the scientific method was taught to students by direct instruction from the teacher and through lab exercises.
4. Students' understanding of the various components of the scientific method was assessed by
   - lab results and write-ups assessed by a common rubric
   - class discussion assessed by teachers' professional judgment
   - a unit test using a common grading scale
   - a common final exam using item analysis by objective and a common grading scale

When aligning curriculum and assessments to standards, teacher teams need to stay focused on the standard. Because most teachers are highly engaged with the content they teach, it is easy for them to lose focus and thus overteach one standard and forget another. It also is common for new topics to be added to the curriculum but never assessed. Teacher teams need to be disciplined about making both the curriculum and the assessments reflect the standards.

Table 3.1.   Course Outline/Curriculum Map for Biology

Course:_____S1053_____

Course Title:_____Biology_____

Course Objective:A. Apply the scientific method to observations made in the labroratory.

_____

_____

Materials Used: (First Semester)_Textbook and workbook for Visualizing Life published by Holt

(Second Semester)_____Same_____

Instructional Objective	Evaluation/Standard
S1053-A1: Explain the difference between hypothesis, theory and fact.	*Lab, workbook, worksheet, test.
S1053-A2: Use the following steps for laboratory experimentation: define the problem, collect information, form a hypothesis, experiment to test the hypothesis, observe and record data and draw a conclusion. (11.A4a - 11.A4f, 13.A.4b, 13.A4d)	*Labs, workbook, class discussion, test.
S1053-A3: Describe how to set up a controlled experiment. (11A.4b) (13.B.4b - "Analyze a particular occupation...." - done throughout the year)	*Lab, workbook, class discussion, test.

Source: DuPage High School District 88, 2002. Reprinted with permission.

Table 3.2. Coding Curriculum Maps to State Standards

Understanding the process of scientific inquiry is a key Illinois Learning Standard in Science. The biology curriculum represented by table 3.1 specifically references the early high school components of this standard and codes the reference in parenthesis in the course outline.

STATE GOAL 11: Understand the processes of scientific inquiry and technological design to investigate questions, conduct experiments, and solve problems.

A. Know and apply the concepts, principles, and processes of scientific inquiry.

Early High School	Late High School
11.A.4a Formulate hypotheses referencing prior research and knowledge.	11.A.5a Formulate hypotheses referencing prior research and knowledge.
11.A.4b Conduct controlled experiments or simulations to test hypotheses.	11.A.5b Design procedures to test the selected hypotheses.
11.A.4c Collect, organize, and analyze data accurately and the selected hypotheses.	11.A.5c Conduct systematic controlled experiments to precisely test the selected hypotheses.
11.A.4d Apply statistical methods to the data to reach and support conclusions.	11.A.5d Apply statistical methods to make predictions and to test the accuracy of results.
11.A.4e Formulate alternative hypotheses to explain unexpected results.	11.A.5e Report, display, and defend the results of investigations to audiences that may include professionals and technical experts.
11.A.4f Using available technology, report, display, and defend to an audience conclusions drawn from investigations.	

Source: From Illinois State Board of Education, 1997, *Illinois Learning Standards*, Goal 11, pp. 32–33.

CURRICULUM CHECKLIST

Not Yet In Progress Completed

1. We have collected materials
   and information to document
   what is currently being taught
   in each grade level and
   subject area. _____ _____ _____

2. We have written common
   curriculum objectives for each
   grade level and subject area. _____ _____ _____

3. We have compared what is
   currently being taught with
   standards and have identified
   gaps and redundancies in our
   local curriculum. _____ _____ _____

4. We have revised the local
   curriculum to eliminate gaps
   and redundancies. _____ _____ _____

5. We have linked our new, local
   curriculum objectives to
   standards. All key standards
   are covered in the new, revised
   curriculum. _____ _____ _____

6. We have examined horizontal
   alignment and pacing issues.
   All teachers at a given grade
   level are following the new,
   common curriculum. _____ _____ _____

7. We have examined vertical alignment so that courses build and prepare students for what is to follow. Vertical gaps and redundancies have been eliminated.   _____   _____   _____

8. We have identified one or more assessments for each curriculum objective.   _____   _____   _____

KEY RESOURCES

Curriculum Maps

Various curriculum map resources are available to schools. In addition to the two samples provided in this chapter, most school districts have a format that is easily adapted to reference and code state standards.

In the past several years curriculum mapping software (e.g., Curriculum Mapper) has become available to schools. These software products provide an online grid into which course objectives, materials, and assessments can be entered. In many cases, state standards can be added by clicking on a specified link.

A number of state websites provide curriculum mapping templates, which schools can use to align the local curriculum with the state standards contained on the templates.

Finally, textbook publishers also are beginning to align textbook content to national and state standards. Publishers provide online curriculum maps for specified textbook series to teachers. These curriculum maps show the standard in a column on the left and then cite the portions of the text where the standard is introduced, practiced, and mastered. In most cases, schools need to add how the students' understanding of the standard is evaluated.

Regardless of the format, schools are encouraged to keep curriculum maps online so that the curriculum may be referenced by teachers, administrators, students, and parents.

Curriculum Resources on State Websites

Now that most states have developed standards, the standards as well as additional resources are posted on state board of education websites. These websites provide not only the standards and curriculum mapping templates but also performance descriptors of specific standards to enable teachers to establish appropriate grade-level performance expectations for students. The review of these performance descriptors is beneficial to grade-level teams as well as vertical articulation teams for identifying desirable learning progressions.

CHAPTER 4

Types of Assessments and Their Purpose

Curriculum answers the question, What should students know? Assessments answer the question, How do we know if they know it? Thus assessments should consist of a series of questions or tasks that are aligned with the common curriculum and measure what students have learned. In general, the questions are content based. Forced choice questions ask students to select a correct answer from a series of possibilities. Performance assessments, such as essays, ask students to demonstrate or show what they have learned. Both types of assessment are based on content the students have been taught.

While the same questions can be used for different assessment purposes, the manner in which the scores are reported and used changes with the purpose of the assessment. Chapter 1 discussed the difference between assessment *of* learning for accountability purposes and assessment *for* learning for purposes of increasing student achievement.

SUMMATIVE ASSESSMENTS

Assessments of learning sum up what a student has learned at a particular point in time. An end-of-course or grade test that is used to determine that a student has mastered the skills and learning necessary to proceed to the next level as well as to assign a final grade may be considered a summative assessment.

Standardized achievement tests also are summative assessments. Schools frequently use the Iowa Test of Basic Skills or the California Achievement Test to measure students' achievement in selected subjects, such as reading, math, and science. State-developed achievement tests based on the state standards also are summative assessments. State tests and other summative assessments give state officials and school administrators a picture of what a student or groups of students have learned; report whether or not students have exceeded, have met, or have fallen below state standards; and are useful for comparisons of students or groups of students.

Summative assessments frequently are normed, standardized tests that are reported in total scores for subject areas such as math, science, or reading. The scores frequently are used to classify individuals or groups of students. Norm referenced tests rank students according to how well they performed in relation to other students. The normed tests are developed by administering the test to a nationwide sample, or norm group. Students taking the test are then ranked according to how well they did in relation to the norm group by being given a score based on one or more of the following methods: (1) grade equivalent score; (2) percentile score, which is the percentage of students a student has scored as well as or better than; (3) assignment to a quartile, which is one of four categories into which percentiles are grouped; and/or (4) assignment to a stanine, which groups students into one of nine categories.

Table 4.1 is an example of how a group of third graders scored on a state reading and math test. If all students in the state mirrored the nation (and the norm group), approximately 25 percent would be in each state quartile. This example shows that students in the school performed below the national norm group in reading and above the national norm group in math.

By aligning the reading and math curricula to state learning standards, schools can improve scores on the state's summative test. With aligned, standards-based curriculum and assessments, they can use local formative assessments to monitor students' learning. By remediating students' gaps and weaknesses in learning before the high-stakes state tests, schools can improve learning for all students and expect scores to be higher on subsequent summative state assessments.

Table 4.1. Sample National Quartile Comparisons

Reading	Quarter 1	Quarter 2	Quarter 3	Quarter 4
School	27%	27%	24%	22%
District	28%	25%	25%	22%
State	21%	21%	25%	33%

Math	Quarter 1	Quarter 2	Quarter 3	Quarter 4
School	13%	27%	32%	28%
District	17%	26%	29%	28%
State	13%	19%	25%	43%

FORMATIVE ASSESSMENTS

Assessments for learning are formative assessments that indicate what a student has learned up to a particular point in time and are used as a guide for further instruction to increase learning. Common formative assessments assess what has been learned by using products and tests that are closely tied to a common curriculum. They usually are teacher-created instruments that are used on a regular basis to measure student progress.

Formative assessments identify the strengths and weaknesses of students and provide valuable information needed to reteach a class, provide special help to individual students, and/or change instructional pacing or materials in the curriculum for future instruction.

Formative assessments frequently are structured in the form of a criterion referenced test (CRT), which tests the criteria or standards a student has been taught and measures how much knowledge a student has gained from instruction. Schools are strongly encouraged to develop standardized CRTs to measure student progress on their standards-based common curricula. These tests are standardized in that they are common exams administered at the same time and under similar conditions to all students taking a particular course or enrolled in the same grade level. They are criterion referenced because they are based on the school's local curriculum objectives, which are linked to state standards. (See the test items section in Key Resources at the end of this chapter.)

Standardized CRT scores usually are reported in percentages, which represent the number of questions the student has answered correctly. The goal of a CRT is to have students score at the upper end of the scale, indicating they have mastered the material that has been taught to them. By developing formative assessments for learning, schools not only will know which curriculum objectives students know and do not know but also will have the ability to gather data to remediate students' weaknesses. Schools should take the following steps to develop formative assessments for learning:

1. *Identify common curricular objectives for each subject at each grade level, as discussed in chapter 3.* This process clarifies the targets of instruction for teachers and provides teachers, students, and parents with the essential information regarding what students are expected to know and be able to do.

2. *Identify methods of assessment for each objective.* Tests should be standardized, common CRTs to provide data for each student in relation to the curriculum objectives. While certain assessment formats lend themselves to assess some objectives better than others, a variety of assessment techniques is desirable and more than one assessment may be used to assess the same objective. It is key, however, that all students receive the same set of common assessments. Note that in table 3.1 students receive multiple and varied assessments in that their understanding of the scientific method is assessed by labs, workbook exercises, and common local assessments. However, all students take each of these assessments so that their learning can be measured.

Assessments need to remain stable over time so that longitudinal data can be collected to assess the impact of changes in instructional practices and materials used. Legal challenges have determined that a test has to match what the students were in fact taught for a test to be fair and valid (*Debra P. v. Turlington* 644 F.2d. 397 U.S. Ct. App. 1981).

3. *Identify the common criteria for each assessment.* Students should know how their work will be judged and the criteria that will

be used. It's a bad joke when teachers say, "What's not covered in class will be covered on the test." Unfortunately for students, the bad joke is too often a reality. What is taught is not reflected by tests, and the content of the test is too often a surprise to students.

Standards, curriculum, instruction, and assessments need to be aligned, and students should know the standards, curriculum objectives, and criteria on which they will be assessed by being exposed to strong and weak examples of student work and by having instruction consciously directed to the criteria. For example, if students are expected to have grammatically perfect writing, they need grammar lessons to remediate areas of weakness before the final writing assessment is given. Students cannot master complex material and skills if standards, curriculum objectives, and criteria are not told to them in advance.

Many states score writing assessments with a rubric that divides the writing into essential traits that can be scored separately. (See the rubrics section in Key Resources.) Table 4.2 provides an example of an analytical trait rubric that is used to score student writing in the following areas: focus, elaboration, organization, integration, and conventions. Different traits could get different scores, which would reveal the strengths and weaknesses of a student's work.

While the state writing assessment is a summative writing assessment, the example in table 4.2 is a "student-friendly" rubric that can be used in formative writing assessments at the local school level. Students using this rubric benefit from learning about the five different scoring areas and understanding their strengths and improving on their weaknesses before the high-stakes summative writing assessment is given. Table 4.3 is an example of a holistic writing rubric, which gives a single score for an entire piece of writing based on an overall impression of a student's work.

4. Pilot the test and then administer it to students. A newly written test should be piloted by a class or group of students to check for poorly written items and the match between what was taught and learned and what was assessed. Once a small group of students has

Table 4.2. Student-Friendly Writing Rubric for Middle School or Junior High

ISAT Student-Friendly Rubric • Middle/Junior High School—Persuasive/Expository

	Focus	Elaboration	Organization	Integration
6	• My subject or position is clear. • I have an engaging opening. • I commented on my subject. • I have an effective closing that ends the paper and ties the whole paper together.	• I used many ways to develop details and support, such as evidence, explanations, and examples. • All of my major points are developed in specific detail. • I used interesting words throughout. • I used details evenly.	• I used appropriate paragraphing. • My writing flows easily from one idea to the next. • I varied my sentence structure and word choice. • All of my paragraphing is purposeful and appropriate. • I tied my sentences and paragraphs together in different ways, such as parallel structure, pronouns, and transitions that indicate time, to make my story flow.	• I have a fully developed paper for my grade level. • I have a clear and developed focus. • I included balanced, specific details. • My sentences and paragraphs fit smoothly together.
5	• I wrote an introduction that makes my subject and position clear. • My closing does more than restate what is in my introduction.	• I used details throughout. • I used several ways to develop details, such as evidence, explanation, and examples. • I used interesting words to add detail and support.	• I used appropriate paragraphing. • My writing flows easily from one idea to the next. • I varied my sentence structure. • Most of my points are appropriately paragraphed. • Some of the word choice and sentence structure I used produces cohesion.	• I have a developed paper for my grade level. • I have a clear and developed focus. • I included specific details. • Some parts of my paper are better than others.

				I tied my sentences and paragraphs together in different ways, such as parallel structure, transitions, pronouns, and repetition.
4	• My subject or position may be introduced by previewing in the introduction. • If I previewed, I talked about only those points I previewed. • My conclusion may be a restatement of the introduction.	• I used many details. I developed most of my main points with specific details. • All of my key points are supported, but some may have more support than others. • I may have used some interesting words.	• Most of my paragraphing is appropriate. • Most of my writing flows from one idea to the next. • I tied my sentences and paragraphs together in different ways.	• My paper is simple, yet clear and appropriate for my grade level. • I included the essentials but nothing more.
3	• My subject or position is identified in a brief opening or at least somewhere in the paper. • I may have talked about more or fewer points than I stated in my introduction. • I may not have a closing. • I may not have written enough.	• Some of the major points in my paper may be developed by specific detail. • I may have included some details that give information beyond the major point.	• I may have used transitions in my paragraphs that confuse my readers. • I used some appropriate paragraphing. • I may have drifted off the subject. • My writing does not flow from one idea to the next.	• My paper is partially developed for my grade level. • My readers may need to figure out what I am writing about because at least one of the features is not complete.
	• My subject and event may be unclear. • I may have been repetitious. • I may have drifted off the subject.	• I used few details. • I may have used a list of details that have some extensions.	• My writing has few appropriate paragraphs. • I drifted way off the subject. • My writing does not flow from one idea to the next.	• I am beginning to use the features of writing. • My paper is confusing. • I may not have written enough.

(continued)

Table 4.2. *(continued)*

ISAT Student-Friendly Rubric • Middle/Junior High School—Persuasive/Expository

	Focus	Elaboration	Organization	Integration
2	• I may have written a response that is not persuasive or expository. • I have written about multiple subjects or positions without tying them together. • I may not have written enough.	• I have only written general details, or I have merely repeated information over and over. • I may not have written enough.	• The sentences in my paragraphs can be reordered without changing the meaning. • My paper is not persuasive or expository. • I may not have written enough.	• I did not write a persuasive or expository paper.
1	• My writing is confusing. • I have not written enough.	• My writing includes no details, • My writing includes no details, or the details I include are confusing. • I have not written enough.	• My writing is confusing. • I may not have written enough.	• My writing is confusing. • I did not fulfill the assignment. • I did not write enough.
	Conventions			Conventions
2	• I have mastered correct use of sentence construction. • I use pronouns correctly. • I have few run-ons or fragments in proportion to the amount I have written. • I have mastered basic use of punctuation and capitalization. • I have mastered correct use of verb tense and subject-verb agreement. • I have few minor and very few major errors in my writing.		1	• The number of errors in my paper interferes with my readers' understanding of what I have written.

Source: Adapted from Illinois State Board of Education, 2003, *Student-Friendly Rubric for Middle/Junior High,* www.isbe.net/assessment/MJHRubricREhtm (accessed March 2005).

Table 4.3. Holistic Writing Rubric

SCORE SIX
A six paper is superior. It does ALL OR MOST of the following:
- Focuses and develops ideas in a sustained and compelling manner, showing creativity and insight
- Clarifies and defends or persuades with precise and relevant evidence; clearly defines and frames issues
- Effectively organizes ideas in a clear, logical, detailed, and coherent manner using appropriate structures to enhance the central idea or theme
- Demonstrates involvement with the text and speaks purposefully to the audience in an appropriate, individualistic, and engaging manner
- Uses multiple sentence structures and word choices effectively and with a sense of control for stylistic effect
- Commits few, if any, errors in standard English rules for grammar/usage and mechanics

SCORE FIVE
A five paper is distinctly above average. It does ALL OR MOST of the following:
- Focuses and develops ideas in an effective and detailed manner
- Defends and/or persuades with important and relevant evidence; defines and frames issues
- Organizes ideas clearly and coherently using structures appropriate to purposes
- Communicates a sense of commitment to the topic and to the audience's involvement
- Uses varied sentence structure and word choice effectively
- Commits few errors in standard English grammar/usage and mechanics

SCORE FOUR
A four paper is adequate. It exhibits ALL OR MOST of the following characteristics:
- Adequately focuses and develops ideas with detail
- Defends and/or persuades with support and clarity, using relevant evidence
- Organizes ideas in a satisfactory manner with adequate coherence and logic
- Uses a voice that is appropriate to audience and purpose
- Uses a variety of sentence structures and word choices, but occasionally displays some wordiness or ineffective diction; sentences may be predictable
- Commits some errors in standard English grammar/usage and mechanics that do not impede meaning; indicates basic understanding of conventions

SCORE THREE
A three paper is inadequate. It is clearly flawed in SOME OR ALL of the following ways:
- Focuses but may not display mature or well-developed content
- Attempts defense or persuasive stance but position is unclear and/or evidence is brief, tangential, or based solely on personal opinion
- Displays minimal organization; contains irrelevancies, digresses, rambles, or lacks logic

(continued)

Table 4.3. (*continued*)

- Lacks sincerity of purpose in the writer's attempt to involve the audience appropriately
- Uses sentence structure and word choice that are somewhat limited, simplistic, mundane, or otherwise inappropriate
- Contains flaws in standard English rules of grammar/usage and mechanics that do not impede meaning; indicates some consistent misunderstanding of the conventions

SCORE TWO

A two paper is very weak. It reveals serious and persistent problems in communications. It compounds the weaknesses of the three paper in SOME OR ALL of the following ways:

- Lacks focus and development; may list items with little or no supporting detail
- Defense or persuasive stance is unclear or absent; evidence is vague or missing.
- Contains serious flaws in structure, organization, and coherence
- Attempts but fails to involve the audience appropriately
- Uses sentence structure and word choice that are highly limited, simplistic, or otherwise inappropriate
- Displays consistent violations in standard English rules of grammar/usage and mechanics that impede understanding

SCORE ONE

A one paper is extremely weak. It has few redeeming qualities. It at least mentions the topic but generally fails to communicate with the reader. It does SOME OR ALL of the following:

- Simply repeats the topic or fails to provide adequate development
- Fails to establish a position and/or develop persuasive view; evidence is not apparent
- Shows almost no structure, organization, or coherence
- Does not address the audience appropriately
- Uses limited and/or immature sentence structure and word choice
- Overwhelms the reader with serious violations of standard English rules grammar/usage and mechanics

---

Source: Adapted from Nevada Department of Education, 2005, *Nevada Writing Holistic Rubric*, www.doe.nv.gov/sca/standards/writing/Holistic%20rubric.html (accessed March 2005).

taken the pilot test, it should be scored and weak items eliminated or replaced.

Rubrics used for performance assessments need to be checked for "interrater reliability," which determines that performances are rated consistently by different teachers (raters) over time. Interrater reliability is strengthened by training teachers or raters using models of performance assessments that produce high, medium, and low scores based on defined criteria.

5. *Test results should undergo item analysis by objective.* In this procedure, test items are tied to a curricular objective using a "pin file." When the test is scored, items for each objective are combined into a percentage score for each objective. By reviewing an item analysis by objective report, one can determine how an individual student, a class, or a group of classes performed on a specific curriculum objective. These reports provide teachers, students, and administrators with valuable information regarding what a student knows and doesn't know.

Table 4.4 illustrates an item analysis by objective report for a biology exam taken by 390 students. The section showing the item analysis for the objective dealing with "applying the scientific method" shows that test items 16 through 28 were written to measure students' understanding of this objective. On this test, students were able to select from choices A, B, C, or D. The asterisk indicates the correct answer. However, the number and percentage of students selecting each answer also is indicated.

This report is valuable for checking understanding of the objective and also for identifying test items that may have been difficult or confusing for students. For example, only 56 percent of the students tested selected the correct response for question 25. While D was the correct answer, 37 percent of the students thought A was the correct answer. These percentages would argue that the teacher should review this question for clarity and consider any instructional information that would have prompted so many students to select A.

6. *Test results should be reviewed by grade-level teacher teams.* While individual teachers can receive an item analysis by objective for their individual classes or for all students taking the test (table 4.4), another useful report for a grade or subject-level team is the standard mastery report (table 4.5). It shows the number and percentage of students mastering curriculum objectives and/or standards. Again using the example of the scientific method objective, the teacher team would see that 381 of the 390 students met or exceeded the expected understanding of the objective and that 9 students need additional help to understand the scientific method.

Table 4.4. Item Analysis by Objective Report for 390 Biology Students

1052 - A: Apply Scientific Method

Item	A	B	C	D	E	Space
#16 -	29 (7%)	42 (11%)	316 (81%)*	2 (1%)	0 (0%)	1 (0%)
#17 -	385 (99%)*	2 (1%)	0 (0%)	3 (1%)	0 (0%)	0 (0%)
#18 -	5 (1%)	12 (3%)	9 (2%)	363 (93%)*	0 (0%)	1 (0%)
#19 -	303 (78%)*	21 (5%)	55 (14%)	10 (3%)	0 (0%)	1 (0%)
#20 -	2 (1%)	347 (89%)*	7 (2%)	33 (8%)	1 (0%)	0 (0%)
#21 -	38 (10%)	1 (0%)	345 (88%)*	7 (2%)	0 (0%)	0 (0%)
#22 -	59 (15%)	283 (73%)*	29 (7%)	20 (5%)	0 (0%)	0 (0%)
#23 -	68 (17%)	299 (77%)*	7 (2%)	18 (5%)	0 (0%)	0 (0%)
#24 -	11 (3%)	4 (1%)	7 (2%)	368 (94%)*	0 (0%)	0 (0%)
#25 -	145 (37%)	20 (5%)	9 (2%)	217 (56%)*	0 (0%)	0 (0%)
#26 -	34 (9%)	5 (1%)	92 (24%)	260 (67%)*	0 (0%)	0 (0%)
#27 -	46 (12%)	6 (2%)	314 (81%)*	25 (6%)	0 (0%)	0 (0%)
#28 -	25 (6%)	304 (78%)*	41 (11%)	21 (5%)	0 (0%)	0 (0%)

1052 - B: Use Lab Eqpt. & Procedure

Item	A	B	C	D	E	Space
#1 -	3 (1%)	3 (1%)	27 (7%)	356 (91%)*	1 (0%)	0 (0%)
#2 -	386 (99%)*	4 (1%)	0 (0%)	0 (0%)	0 (0%)	0 (0%)
#3 -	2 (1%)	362 (93%)*	1 (0%)	24 (6%)	0 (0%)	1 (0%)
#4 -	33 (8%)	0 (0%)	0 (0%)	357 (92%)*	0 (0%)	1 (0%)
#5 -	309 (79%)*	79 (20%)	0 (0%)	1 (0%)	0 (0%)	1 (0%)
#6 -	77 (20%)	6 (2%)	287 (74%)*	18 (5%)	2 (1%)	2 (1%)
#7 -	14 (4%)	47 (12%)	22 (6%)	306 (78%)*	2 (1%)	2 (1%)
#8 -	6 (2%)	320 (82%)*	17 (4%)	49 (13%)	0 (0%)	0 (0%)
#9 -	298 (76%)*	19 (5%)	59 (15%)	13 (3%)	0 (0%)	2 (1%)
#10 -	0 (0%)	2 (1%)	2 (1%)	1 (0%)	387 (99%)*	0 (0%)
#11 -	70 (18%)	285 (73%)*	33 (8%)	5 (1%)	0 (0%)	0 (0%)
#12 -	338 (87%)*	21 (5%)*	12 (3%)	19 (5%)	0 (0%)	0 (0%)
#13 -	197 (51%)*	195 (50%)	0 (0%)	0 (0%)	0 (0%)	0 (0%)
#14 -	383 (98%)*	9 (2%)	0 (0%)	0 (0%)	0 (0%)	0 (0%)
#15 -	25 (6%)	365 (94%)*	1 (0%)	0 (0%)	0 (0%)	0 (0%)
#29 -	14 (4%)	48 (12%)	6 (2%)	323 (83%)*	0 (0%)	0 (0%)
#30 -	3 (1%)	24 (6%)	349 (89%)*	14 (4%)	0 (0%)	0 (0%)

The Assessor by Software America, Inc.

Source: DuPage High School District 88, 2001. Copyright © Software America, Inc. (800-860-8843). Reprinted with permission.

7. Based on test results, teachers should decide to reteach the curriculum objectives on which the class did not perform well, provide special help to individual students, and/or make adjustments to the curriculum and/or instruction. It is key that individual teachers and teacher teams take time to review test results. In this way, common assessments actually become assessments for learning in that ad-

Table 4.5.   Standard Mastery Report for 390 Biology Students

	Forced Choice Mastery		Performance Mastery		Total Mastery	
Expected.						
Overall Pass/ Fail						
---------> EXCEEDS	266	68% (91 of 130)	0	0% (0 of 0)	266	68%
---------> MEETS	118	30% (65 of 130)	0	0% (0 of 0)	118	30%
---------> DOES NOT MEET	6	2%	0	0%	6	2%
S1051 - OVERALL - (98%) 384 of 390 Students have Mastered this COURSE OBJECTIVES. 0%						
Expected.						
Apply Scientific Method						
---------> EXCEEDS	291	75% (9 of 13)	0	0% (0 of 0)	291	75%
---------> MEETS	90	23% (7 of 13)	0	0% (0 of 0)	90	23%
---------> DOES NOT MEET	9	2%	0	0%	9	2%
S1052 - A - (98%) 381 of 390 Students have Mastered this COURSE OBJECTIVES. 0%						
Expected.						
Use Lab Eqpt. & Procedure						
---------> EXCEEDS	356	91% (12 of 17)	0	0% (0 of 0)	356	91%
---------> MEETS	28	7% (9 of 17)	0	0% (0 of 0)	28	7%
---------> DOES NOT MEET	6	2%	0	0%	6	2%
S1052 - B - (98%) 384 of 390 Students have Mastered this COURSE OBJECTIVES. 0%						
Expected.						
Use Chemistry to Relate						
---------> EXCEEDS	232	59% (14 of 20)	0	0% (0 of 0)	232	59%
---------> MEETS	121	31% (10 of 20)	0	0% (0 of 0)	121	31%
---------> DOES NOT MEET	37	9%	0	0%	37	9%
S1052 - C - (91%) 353 of 390 Students have Mastered this COURSE OBJECTIVES. 0%						
Expected.						
Cell Parts & Functions						
---------> EXCEEDS	226	58% (7 of 10)	0	0% (0 of 0)	226	58%
---------> MEETS	89	23% (5 of 10)	0	0% (0 of 0)	89	23%
---------> DOES NOT MEET	75	19%	0	0%	75	19%
S1052 - D - (81%) 315 of 390 Students have Mastered this COURSE OBJECTIVES. 0%						
Expected.						
Cell Physiology						
---------> EXCEEDS	134	34% (14 of 20)	0	0% (0 of 0)	134	34%
---------> MEETS	161	41% (10 of 20)	0	0% (0 of 0)	161	41%
---------> DOES NOT MEET	95	24%	0	0%	95	24%
S1052 - E - (76%) 295 of 390 Students have Mastered this COURSE OBJECTIVES. 0%						

The Assessor by Software America, Inc.

Source: DuPage High School District 88, 2001. Copyright © Software America, Inc. (800-860-8843). Reprinted with permission.

ministrators and teachers ascertain what students still need to learn and thus gain information about what needs to be retaught or changed.

Chapter 2 explained how the data from math tests motivated one school to improve students' skills and understanding of measurement by purchasing new textbooks and additional instructional supplies (e.g., rulers and tape measures) and spending more instructional time on the topic of measurement in order to increase students' skills and test scores in the area of measurement. This is an example of how a formative assessment was used to change curriculum and instructional practices.

Data from a formative assessment also may stimulate the need to reteach a class, a group of students, or an individual. Albert Shanker (cited in Wiggins 1993, 262) has remarked that "if a doctor's prescription and advice fail to work for a particular patient, the doctor is obligated to try an alternative approach." Most good teachers also understand the need to have alternative approaches to subject matter and the need to reteach.

For example, English teachers will frequently reteach points of grammar via "target lessons" when several students make a particular grammatical error. They begin with a short target lesson to the entire class. When a smaller number of students continue to make the same error, they keep them after class a few minutes for another target lesson, this time using different examples. Usually that remedies the problem. Sometimes, however, a student will continue to make errors. Donna, a high school freshman, continued to use "yous." Meeting with her during her lunch period, her teacher explained that "yous" simply was not correct English usage. Meeting one-on-one gave the student the freedom to ask, "Then what do you say when there is more that one 'you?' You've got to say 'yous.'" After more conversation, the teacher explained with eventual success that in English "you" was used for both the singular and plural pronoun and did not hear her use "yous" again.

THE COMPLEMENTARY ROLE OF FORMATIVE AND SUMMATIVE ASSESSMENTS

Formative assessments and summative assessments should complement each other. If used correctly, formative assessments will provide teachers with data to help students increase their learning and thus help students achieve a higher score on a high-stakes summative assessment such as the state test of standards, and summative assessments will provide assurances to schools, parents, and community members that the local curriculum and assessments are aligned with standards and levels of achievement outside the district. In other words, formative assessments assess the local curriculum objectives that are being taught to students and provide data that show what students have or have not learned. Normed summative assessments assess students' knowledge in given subject areas and provide data that show how individuals or groups of students rank or compare with others in their local school, state, or nation. (See table 4.1.)

In terms of accountability, state tests are summative assessments validating that schools, teachers, local curriculum, instructional practices, and local assessments are preparing students to meet and exceed state standards as well as the challenges of the future. However, accountability at the local school level is strongly influenced by the school's ability to collect and use local test data to help students learn. Thus the primary force in accountability is not the state or the federal government but the local school administrator. He or she is responsible for promoting an instructional program built on common curriculum and assessments that produce reliable data so that teachers have the means to guide each student's learning experiences.

Using a combination of formative and summative assessments provides teachers and administrators with powerful means to increase student achievement. Local formative assessments reveal students' strengths and weaknesses and provide valuable data to reteach students and remediate their weaknesses before they take high-stakes summative assessments. Good local assessment practices also provide multiple and varied opportunities for students to display and document what they know and what they don't know.

A variety of formative and summative assessment techniques should be used to provide a comprehensive picture of what students know. Alfred Binet (as cited in Wiggins 1993, 13), who pioneered intelligence testing, also encouraged numerous tests to create a more valid picture, stating that "one test signifies nothing . . . but five or six tests signify something. And that is so true that one might almost say, it matters very little what the tests are so long as they are numerous." There are many types of assessments, and the assessment type must be matched with the curriculum objectives to measure what students have learned. It is also important that the test giver understand the purpose of the assessment and the data it produces.

TYPES OF ASSESSMENTS

Standardized tests are constructed and administered so that students are assessed under uniform conditions and consequently test performances may be compared and are not influenced by differing conditions. Both formative and summative tests may be standardized, and both norm referenced and criterion referenced tests may be standardized. Depending on test content, a standardized test may or may not test standards or curriculum objectives, which define knowledge and skills to be taught and learned as a result of instruction.

Criterion referenced tests assess students' progress toward specific criteria or content standards that were the focus of instruction. Rather than ranking a student with a norm group, a CRT measures mastery of the curriculum objectives by a student or group of students. Scores are usually reported in percentage of questions answered correctly.

Norm referenced tests assess students' knowledge of subject matter in relation to the knowledge of the norm group, which is a random sample of students chosen by the test developer to establish an average score. Students taking the test are then ranked according to how well they did in relation to the norm group by being given a score based on one or more of the following methods: (1) grade equivalent score; (2) a percentile score, which is the percentage of students a student has scored as well as or better than; (3) assignment to a quartile, which is one of four categories into which percentiles are grouped; and/or (4) assignment to a stanine, which groups students into one of nine categories.

Selected response/forced choice/objective tests frequently are used to assess students' knowledge of factual information. Multiple choice, true-false, and matching are common formats for these tests, and they require students to select a response from a list of choices or supply a brief answer. Test items may be aligned with standards or curriculum objectives; item analysis by standard or curriculum objective, using a CRT format, can be used to provide valuable information regarding student progress toward curriculum objectives.

Norm referenced tests (NRTs) usually are composed of selected response items to measure students' knowledge in specific content areas. In the case of an NRT, items are scored and total scores are compared to the performance of the norm group. For items on either a CRT or NRT, student responses can be scored quickly and objectively as there is usually one best answer.

Performance tests assess students' knowledge and skills by requiring them to construct a product (e.g., a written report or a project) or performance (e.g., a speech or laboratory experiment). These tests do not have one correct answer and are judged on known criteria, which usually are included in a rubric that defines both the content and the quality of the performance.

A performance test may be a CRT in that the criteria are the basis for instruction and the grading criteria for the rubric. Though less likely, due to the complexity of scoring, a performance test may also be a rubric-graded normed test, where the student's score is compared to the scores of the norm group.

The key in developing a system to enhance achievement is to decide what students should know and then teach and assess those objectives. Too often schools fail to link their assessments to the curriculum objectives and standards and, as a result, have no idea if students are being taught the curriculum and/or if they are learning it.

ASSESSMENT CHECKLIST

	Not Yet	In Progress	Completed
1. Key common assessments have been written by grade/subject-level teams.	_____	_____	_____
2. Common assessments are criterion referenced and aligned with the local curriculum objectives and a clearly defined set of standards.	_____	_____	_____
3. Common assessments are formative and provide teachers with useful data regarding what students do and do not know.	_____	_____	_____
4. Common assessments provide data useful in assessing curriculum objectives, teaching methods, and instructional materials.	_____	_____	_____
5. Common assessments have been piloted to eliminate bias and poor questions and to maximize alignment to the curriculum.	_____	_____	_____

6. Common assessments
   undergo item analysis by
   curriculum objective, and
   reports are provided to
   teachers and administrators
   on a timely basis.   _____   _____   _____

7. Common assessment
   results are analyzed by
   grade/subject-level teams
   to identify areas for
   curricular revision and
   areas for reteaching and
   individual student
   remediation.   _____   _____   _____

KEY RESOURCES

Rubrics

State board of education websites often contain scoring rubrics for state assessments in writing. These rubrics are a valuable resource for teachers because they provide the criteria, scoring values, and terminology used by the individuals who score the state writing samples.

In addition to the official rubrics, many state websites also contain "student-friendly" rubrics that can be used by teachers and students to help students understand the strengths and weaknesses of their own writing. The greatest value in using a state-developed rubric for writing is that it helps teachers and students develop a common vocabulary about writing and helps define a progression in writing development grade by grade.

Test Items

Many state websites also provide banks of test items that are aligned with state standards. These item banks are helpful to teachers, not only because they provide questions, but also because they provide the level of difficulty and specificity students are expected to know on the state test of standards. Test item banks aligned with standards also may be purchased from commercial test developers.

Under no circumstances should teachers use actual test questions from current state tests for teaching examples, homework, or drills. Most states release old tests for practice or provide similar questions on their websites.

CHAPTER 5

Gathering and Analyzing Meaningful Data

Once the curriculum and assessments have been aligned with the standards, the question, What should students know? has been answered. The next step is to answer the question, How do you know if students know it? While most schools engage in testing students, testing alone doesn't answer the question, How do you know if students know it? Testing provides a general answer regarding whether or not students understood the material tested, but it too often signals to both teachers and students that the unit of study is over, and it's time to move on to new material. If schools are going to improve student achievement, formative common local assessment results need to be analyzed to see what students have learned and what they haven't learned so that steps to improve learning may be taken.

Although test analysis may be done by hand, modern assessment software provides teachers, students, and administrators with valuable test analyses quickly and efficiently. (See the assessment software in Key Resources at the end of the chapter.) After a formative common local assessment has been administered and scored, computerized analysis should be performed to determine what students do and do not know and to improve the test by discarding poor or confusing test questions.

STEPS FOR TEST ANALYSIS

1. Align the curriculum objectives to the standards.

2. Write test items to measure students' knowledge of each of the curriculum objectives. Approximately the same number of test items should be written for each objective, though more items could be written for important objectives.

3. As the test is being written, align the test items with the curriculum objectives. This alignment will allow the test writers to see how many questions have been written for each objective and will also allow the creation of an item analysis by objective report. This report will show teachers and students which objectives students understand and which they do not. Table 5.1 is an example of a pin file created for an algebra test. It shows that questions 1–19 test the objective "organize and analyze data by applying statistical methods," that questions 20–39 test students' understanding of and ability to "graph linear equations in two variables," that questions 43–51 test students' ability to "solve word problems by writing and solving an equation," that questions 52–66 test students' ability to "solve problems involving percents and proportions," and that questions 67–71 test students' ability to "apply geometric knowledge of polynomials including formulas for perimeter and area."

4. Administer the common assessment to students. Before a key common assessment is given to a large number of students, it is a good idea to pilot the test with a small number of students. This will identify questions that are poorly written or confusing to students. These questions should be revised before the test is administered to a large group of students.

5. Score the test and request the reports. Most assessment software programs provide a variety of reports. *Alphabetical student results* reports (table 5.2) list a class or group of students alphabetically by name, tell the number of questions answered correctly, and assign a grade based on the agreed-on grading scale.

Item analysis of the test questions for a given group of students (table 5.3) shows the correct answer with the asterisk and the number and percentage of students selecting each answer. The report can be run for an individual class or for the entire group of students taking the test. This report is useful for identifying test items that were

Table 5.1. Pin File for Local Assessment in Algebra

The following format is used to align test items with the curriculum objectives and the state standards in math.

Course Objective Response Key:

Course Objective No. 1: Organize and analyze data by applying statistical methods. Proficiency: 60%

Item No.	Answer	Item No.	Answer	Item No.	Answer	Item No.	Answer
1	B	6	D	11	A	16	A
2	D	7	C	12	C	17	D
3	C	8	A	13	D	18	B
4	B	9	C	14	B	19	D
5	C	10	C	15	A		

Total No. of Items: 19

Course Objective No. 2: Graph linear equations in two variables. Proficiency: 60%

Item No.	Answer	Item No.	Answer	Item No.	Answer	Item No.	Answer
20	B	25	B	30	B	35	A
21	C	26	D	31	A	36	A
22	C	27	D	32	B	37	A
23	A	28	A	33	A	38	A
24	D	29	D	34	B	39	D
						40	A
						41	B
						42	C

Total No. of Items: 23

Course Objective No. 3: Solve word problems by writing and solving an equation. Proficiency: 60%

Item No.	Answer	Item No.	Answer
43	B	48	C
44	D	49	A
45	B	50	C
46	D	51	C
47	A		

Total No. of Items: 9

Course Objective No. 4: Solve problems involving percents and proportions. Proficiency: 60%

Item No.	Answer	Item No.	Answer	Item No.	Answer
52	A	57	C	62	C
53	D	58	A	63	A
54	C	59	B	64	D
55	B	60	A	65	C
56	D	61	B	66	B

Total No. of Items: 15

Course Objective No. 5: Apply geometric knowledge of polynomials including formulas for perimeter and area. Proficiency: 60%

Item No.	Answer
67	C
68	D
69	A
70	B
71	C

Total No. of Items: 5

The Assessor Course Objective Response Key

Source: DuPage High School District 88, 2002. Reprinted with permission.

Table 5.2.   Alphabetical Student Results for 23 Students on a Forced-Choice Test

Student Name	Performance	Forced Choice	Total	Grade	
Carlos, Juan	0 of 0	54 of 71	76	76%	C
Davis, Sally	0 of 0	47 of 71	66	66%	D
Ease, Linda	0 of 0	64 of 71	90	90%	A
Edwards, Jennifer	0 of 0	49 of 71	69	69%	D
Force, Jennifer	0 of 0	53 of 71	75	75%	C
Gates, Henry	0 of 0	55 of 71	77	77%	C
Gregory, Russell	0 of 0	59 of 71	83	83%	B
Hicks, Joseph	0 of 0	57 of 71	80	80%	B
Jones, Abby	0 of 0	47 of 71	66	66%	D
King, Daniel	0 of 0	60 of 71	84	84%	B
Layne, Nicole	0 of 0	56 of 71	79	79%	C
Lowe, Irma	0 of 0	52 of 71	73	73%	C
Monroe, Ray	0 of 0	43 of 71	61	61%	D
Moses, Javier	0 of 0	51 of 71	72	72%	C
Nance, William	0 of 0	55 of 71	77	77%	C
Norris, Leticia	0 of 0	57 of 71	80	80%	B
Olsen, Monica	0 of 0	40 of 71	56	56%	F
Pope, Melissa	0 of 0	52 of 71	73	73%	C
Royce, Joe	0 of 0	50 of 71	70	70%	C
Smith, Paul	0 of 0	22 of 71	31	31%	F
Tate, Ronda	0 of 0	43 of 71	61	61%	D
Todd, Angelica	0 of 0	49 of 71	69	69%	D
Wilson, Betty	0 of 0	36 of 71	51	51%	F
23 Student Average	0 of 0	50 of 71	70	70%	C

The Assessor by Software America, Inc.

Source: From DuPage High School District 88, 2000. Copyright © Software America, Inc. (800-860-8843). Reprinted with permission.

difficult for students because they didn't understand the material or for identifying poorly written test items. Questions that students didn't understand because they didn't understand the material or because the test item was poorly written will have a high percentage of wrong answers. The correct answer, marked with the asterisk, will have a low percentage.

Item analysis by objective groups test questions by curriculum objective and shows the correct answer as well as the percentage of students selecting each answer (table 5.4). The notation in parenthe-

Table 5.3. Item Analysis for 23 Students on a 71-Question Forced Choice Test

Item	A	B	C	D	E	Space	Diff	Discrim
#1 -	0 (0%)	18 (78%)*	5 (22%)	0 (0%)	0 (0%)	0 (0%)	0.783	-0.500
#2 -	4 (17%)	0 (0%)	0 (0%)	19 (83%)*	0 (0%)	0 (0%)	0.826	-0.333
#3 -	0 (0%)	2 (9%)	18 (78%)*	3 (13%)	0 (0%)	0 (0%)	0.783	+0.167
#4 -	2 (9%)	17 (74%)*	3 (13%)	1 (4%)	0 (0%)	1 (4%)	0.739	-0.667
#5 -	0 (0%)	3 (13%)	17 (74%)*	2 (9%)	0 (0%)	1 (4%)	0.739	0.000
#6 -	2 (9%)	1 (4%)	0 (0%)	19 (83%)*	0 (0%)	1 (4%)	0.739	-0.167
#7 -	2 (9%)	2 (9%)	19 (83%)*	0 (0%)	0 (0%)	0 (0%)	0.826	-0.500
#8 -	14 (61%)*	2 (9%)	3 (13%)	4 (17%)	0 (0%)	0 (0%)	0.609	0.000
#9 -	0 (0%)	2 (9%)	21 (91%)*	0 (0%)	0 (0%)	0 (0%)	0.913	-0.333
#10 -	2 (9%)	4 (17%)	16 (70%)*	1 (4%)	0 (0%)	0 (0%)	0.696	-0.167
#11 -	7 (30%)*	3 (13%)	1 (4%)	11 (48%)	0 (0%)	1 (4%)	0.304	+0.167
#12 -	1 (4%)	3 (13%)	19 (83%)*	0 (0%)	0 (0%)	0 (0%)	0.826	-0.167
#13 -	0 (0%)	0 (0%)	0 (0%)	23 (100%)*	0 (0%)	0 (0%)	1.000	0.000
#14 -	1 (4%)	20 (87%)*	2 (9%)	0 (0%)	0 (0%)	0 (0%)	0.870	-0.167
#15 -	21 (91%)*	0 (0%)	2 (9%)	0 (0%)	0 (0%)	0 (0%)	0.913	+0.167
#16 -	17 (74%)*	0 (0%)	1 (4%)	5 (22%)	0 (0%)	0 (0%)	0.739	+0.333
#17 -	4 (17%)	13 (57%)*	4 (17%)	2 (9%)	0 (0%)	0 (0%)	0.565	+0.167
#18 -	2 (9%)	1 (4%)	2 (9%)	18 (78%)*	0 (0%)	0 (0%)	0.783	-0.500
#19 -	1 (4%)	14 (61%)*	5 (22%)	3 (13%)	0 (0%)	0 (0%)	0.609	+0.167
#20 -	1 (4%)	16 (70%)*	4 (17%)	1 (4%)	0 (0%)	1 (4%)	0.696	0.000
#21 -	2 (9%)	0 (0%)	14 (61%)*	5 (22%)	0 (0%)	2 (9%)	0.609	-0.667
#22 -	1 (4%)	1 (4%)	15 (65%)*	6 (26%)	0 (0%)	0 (0%)	0.652	-0.500
#23 -	17 (74%)*	3 (13%)	0 (0%)	2 (9%)	0 (0%)	1 (4%)	0.739	0.000
#24 -	0 (0%)	3 (13%)	0 (0%)	20 (87%)*	0 (0%)	0 (0%)	0.870	-0.500
#25 -	1 (4%)	18 (78%)*	0 (0%)	4 (17%)	0 (0%)	0 (0%)	0.783	-0.333
#26 -	2 (9%)	5 (22%)	2 (9%)	14 (61%)*	0 (0%)	0 (0%)	0.609	-0.333
#27 -	1 (4%)	0 (0%)	1 (4%)	21 (91%)*	0 (0%)	0 (0%)	0.913	-0.167
#28 -	19 (83%)*	1 (4%)	3 (13%)	0 (0%)	0 (0%)	0 (0%)	0.826	-0.167
#29 -	0 (0%)	1 (4%)	4 (17%)	18 (78%)*	0 (0%)	0 (0%)	0.783	+0.167
#30 -	0 (0%)	15 (65%)*	5 (22%)	3 (13%)	0 (0%)	0 (0%)	0.652	-0.667
#31 -	11 (48%)*	2 (9%)	9 (39%)	1 (4%)	0 (0%)	0 (0%)	0.478	-0.167
#32 -	5 (22%)	14 (61%)*	2 (9%)	2 (9%)	0 (0%)	0 (0%)	0.609	-0.667
#33 -	19 (83%)*	2 (9%)	1 (4%)	1 (4%)	0 (0%)	0 (0%)	0.826	-0.333
#34 -	0 (0%)	22 (96%)*	0 (0%)	1 (4%)	0 (0%)	0 (0%)	0.957	-0.167
#35 -	19 (83%)*	1 (4%)	1 (4%)	2 (9%)	0 (0%)	0 (0%)	0.826	-0.500
#36 -	20 (87%)*	2 (9%)	0 (0%)	1 (4%)	0 (0%)	0 (0%)	0.870	-0.167
#37 -	16 (70%)*	0 (0%)	1 (4%)	6 (26%)	0 (0%)	0 (0%)	0.696	-0.333
#38 -	14 (61%)*	5 (22%)	1 (4%)	3 (13%)	0 (0%)	0 (0%)	0.609	-1.000
#39 -	2 (9%)	9 (39%)	1 (4%)	11 (48%)*	0 (0%)	0 (0%)	0.478	-.0500

(continued)

Table 5.3. (*continued*)

#40 -	20 (87%)*	1 (4%)	0 (0%)	3 (13%)	0 (0%)	0 (0%)	0.870	-0.333
#41 -	2 (9%)	17 (74%)*	1 (4%)	3 (13%)	0 (0%)	0 (0%)	0.739	+0.167
#42 -	2 (9%)	1 (4%)	18 (78%)*	2 (9%)	0 (0%)	0 (0%)	0.783	-0.167
#43 -	0 (0%)	22 (96%)*	0 (0%)	1 (4%)	0 (0%)	0 (0%)	0.957	-0.167
#44 -	2 (9%)	0 (0%)	3 (13%)	18 (78%)*	0 (0%)	0 (0%)	0.783	-0.167
#45 -	6 (26%)	15 (65%)*	1 (4%)	1 (4%)	0 (0%)	0 (0%)	0.652	0.000
#46 -	2 (9%)	6 (26%)	10 (43%)	6 (26%)*	0 (0%)	0 (0%)	0.261	-0.167
#47 -	14 (61%)*	2 (9%)	2 (9%)	5 (22%)	0 (0%)	0 (0%)	0.609	-0.167
#48 -	2 (9%)	2 (9%)	18 (78%)*	1 (4%)	0 (0%)	0 (0%)	0.783	-0.167
#49 -	13 (57%)*	2 (9%)	4 (17%)	5 (22%)	0 (0%)	0 (0%)	0.565	-0.167
#50 -	2 (9%)	2 (9%)	14 (61%)*	4 (17%)	0 (0%)	0 (0%)	0.609	+0.167
#51 -	2 (9%)	7 (30%)	12 (52%)*	2 (9%)	0 (0%)	0 (0%)	0.522	-0.167
#52 -	22 (96%)*	1 (4%)	0 (0%)	0 (0%)	0 (0%)	0 (0%)	0.957	-0.167
#53 -	2 (9%)	3 (13%)	7 (30%)	11 (48%)*	0 (0%)	0 (0%)	0.478	-0.833
#54 -	0 (0%)	3 (13%)	18 (78%)*	2 (9%)	0 (0%)	0 (0%)	0.783	-0.500
#55 -	3 (13%)	14 (61%)*	2 (9%)	4 (22%)	0 (0%)	0 (0%)	0.609	-0.500
#56 -	2 (9%)	2 (9%)	2 (9%)	17 (74%)*	0 (0%)	0 (0%)	0.739	-0.333
#57 -	0 (0%)	2 (9%)	21 (91%)*	0 (0%)	0 (0%)	0 (0%)	0.913	-0.333
#58 -	14 (61%)*	1 (4%)	1 (4%)	7 (30%)	0 (0%)	0 (0%)	0.609	-0.667
#59 -	1 (4%)	21 (91%)*	1 (4%)	0 (0%)	0 (0%)	0 (0%)	0.913	-0.167
#60 -	15 (65%)*	3 (13%)	3 (13%)	2 (9%)	0 (0%)	0 (0%)	0.652	-0.167
#61 -	3 (13%)	9 (39%)*	8 (35%)	3 (13%)	0 (0%)	0 (0%)	0.391	-0.667
#62 -	2 (9%)	4 (17%)	17 (74%)*	0 (0%)	0 (0%)	0 (0%)	0.739	0.000
#63 -	13 (57%)*	3 (13%)	5 (22%)	1 (4%)	0 (0%)	1 (4%)	0.565	-0.333
#64 -	0 (0%)	4 (17%)	9 (39%)	10 (43%)*	0 (0%)	0 (0%)	0.435	-0.333
#65 -	4 (17%)	2 (9%)	16 (70%)*	1 (4%)	0 (0%)	0 (0%)	0.696	-0.667
#66 -	6 (26%)	17 (74%)*	0 (0%)	0 (0%)	0 (0%)	0 (0%)	0.739	0.000
#67 -	4 (17%)	1 (4%)	18 (78%)*	0 (0%)	0 (0%)	0 (0%)	0.783	-0.500
#68 -	7 (30%)	1 (4%)	0 (0%)	15 (65%)*	0 (0%)	0 (0%)	0.652	-0.333
#69 -	12 (52%)*	10 (43%)	1 (4%)	0 (0%)	0 (0%)	0 (0%)	0.522	0.167
#70 -	3 (13%)	16 (70%)*	3 (13%)	1 (4%)	0 (0%)	0 (0%)	0.696	-0.333
#71 -	6 (26%)	6 (26%)	8 (35%)*	3 (13%)	0 (0%)	0 (0%)	0.348	0.000

Mean: 50.04
Median: 52.00
Variance: 81.50
Standard Deviation: 9.03

Split-Half Pearson P.M.C.C: 0.72
Split-Half Spearman-Brown: 0.84
Kuder-Richardson Formula 20: 0.85
Kuder-Richardson Formula 21: 0.83

The Assessor by Software America, Inc.

Source: From DuPage High School District 88, 2000. Copyright © Software America, Inc. (800-860-8843). Reprinted with permission.

ses indicates the state standard to which the objective and the test items are aligned. This report is useful in determining which of the curriculum objectives students have learned and which they have not. Table 5.4 shows a report run for twenty-three students (one class) taking a semester algebra exam.

By reviewing this report, the teacher can see which objectives students understood and which they did not. If an entire class scores

Table 5.4. Item Analysis by Objective for 23 Students on a 71-Question Forced Choice Test

M1173 - 06: Solve problems involving percents and proportions.
(S.6.D.4, S.7.C.4b, S.9.A.4a, S.10.A.4a)

Item	A	B	C	D	E	Space
#52 -	22 (96%)*	1 (4%)	0 (0%)	0 (0%)	0 (0%)	0 (0%)
#53 -	2 (9%)	3 (13%)	7 (30%)	11 (48%)*	0 (0%)	0 (0%)
#54 -	0 (0%)	3 (13%)	18 (78%)*	2 (9%)	0 (0%)	0 (0%)
#55 -	3 (13%)	14 (61%)*	2 (9%)	4 (17%)	0 (0%)	0 (0%)
#56 -	2 (9%)	2 (9%)	2 (9%)	17 (74%)*	0 (0%)	0 (0%)
#57 -	0 (0%)	2 (9%)	21 (91%)*	0 (0%)	0 (0%)	0 (0%)
#58 -	14 (61%)*	1 (4%)	1 (4%)	7 (30%)	0 (0%)	0 (0%)
#59 -	1 (4%)	21 (91%)*	1 (4%)	0 (0%)	0 (0%)	0 (0%)
#60 -	15 (65%)*	3 (13%)	3 (13%)	2 (9%)	0 (0%)	0 (0%)
#61 -	3 (13%)	9 (39%)*	8 (35%)	3 (13%)	0 (0%)	0 (0%)
#62 -	2 (9%)	4 (17%)	17 (74%)*	0 (0%)	0 (0%)	0 (0%)
#63 -	13 (57)*	3 (13%)	5 (22%)	1 (4%)	0 (0%)	1 (4%)
#64 -	0 (0%)	4 (17%)	9 (39%)	10 (43%)*	0 (0%)	0 (0%)
#65 -	4 (17%)	2 (9%)	16 (70%)*	1 (4%)	0 (0%)	0 (0%)
#66 -	6 (26%)	17 (74%)*	0 (0%)	0 (0%)	0 (0%)	0 (0%)

M1173 - 08: Solve word problems by writing and solving an equation.
(S.6.B.4, S.6.C.4)

Item	A	B	C	D	E	Space
#43 -	0 (0%)	22 (96%)*	0 (0%)	1 (4%)	0 (0%)	0 (0%)
#44 -	2 (9%)	0 (0%)	3 (13%)	18 (78%)*	0 (0%)	0 (0%)
#45 -	6 (26%)	15 (65%)*	1 (4%)	1 (4%)	0 (0%)	0 (0%)
#46 -	2 (9%)	6 (26%)	10 (43%)	6 (26%)*	0 (0%)	0 (0%)
#47 -	14 (61%)*	2 (9%)	2 (9%)	5 (22%)	0 (0%)	0 (0%)
#48 -	2 (9%)	2 (9%)	18 (78%)*	1 (4%)	0 (0%)	0 (0%)
#49 -	13 (57%)*	2 (9%)	4 (17%)	5 (22%)	0 (0%)	0 (0%)
#50 -	2 (9%)	2 (9%)	14 (61%)*	4 (17%)	0 (0%)	1 (4%)
#51 -	2 (9%)	7 (30%)	12 (52%)*	2 (9%)	0 (0%)	0 (0%)

M1173 - 10: Graph linear equations in two variables.
(S.8.C.4a, S.8.D.4, S.9.B.4)

Item	A	B	C	D	E	Space
#20 -	1 (4%)	16 (70%)*	4 (17%)	1 (4%)	0 (0%)	1 (4%)
#21 -	2 (9%)	0 (0%)	14 (61%)*	5 (22%)	0 (0%)	2 (9%)
#22 -	1 (4%)	1 (4%)	15 (65%)*	6 (26%)	0 (0%)	0 (0%)
#23 -	17 (74%)*	3 (13%)	0 (0%)	2 (9%)	0 (0%)	1 (4%)
#24 -	0 (0%)	3 (13%)	0 (0%)	20 (87%)*	0 (0%)	0 (0%)
#25 -	1 (4%)	18 (78%)*	0 (0%)	4 (17%)	0 (0%)	0 (0%)
#26 -	2 (9%)	5 (22%)	2 (9%)	14 (61%)*	0 (0%)	0 (0%)
#27 -	1 (4%)	0 (0%)	1 (4%)	21 (91%)*	0 (0%)	0 (0%)

The Assessor by Software America, Inc.

Source: DuPage High School District 88, 2000. Copyright © Software America, Inc. (800-860-8843). Reprinted with permission.

Table 5.4. (continued)

	A	B	C	D	E	Space
#28 -	19 (83%)*	1 (4%)	3 (13%)	0 (0%)	0 (0%)	0 (0%)
#29 -	0 (0%)	1 (4%)	4 (17%)	18 (78%)*	0 (0%)	0 (0%)
#30 -	0 (0%)	15 (65%)*	5 (22%)	3 (13%)	0 (0%)	0 (0%)
#31 -	11 (48%)*	2 (9%)	9 (39%)	1 (4%)	0 (0%)	0 (0%)
#32 -	5 (22%)	14 (61%)*	2 (9%)	2 (9%)	0 (0%)	0 (0%)
#33 -	19 (83%)*	2 (9%)	1 (4%)	1 (4%)	0 (0%)	0 (0%)
#34 -	0 (0%)	22 (96%)*	0 (0%)	1 (4%)	0 (0%)	0 (0%)
#35 -	19 (83%)*	1 (4%)	1 (4%)	2 (9%)	0 (0%)	0 (0%)
#36 -	20 (87%)*	2 (9%)	0 (0%)	1 (4%)	0 (0%)	0 (0%)
#37 -	16 (70%)*	0 (0%)	1 (4%)	6 (26%)	0 (0%)	0 (0%)
#38 -	14 (61%)*	5 (22%)	1 (4%)	3 (13%)	0 (0%)	0 (0%)
#39 -	2 (9%)	9 (39%)	1 (4%)	11 (48%)*	0 (0%)	0 (0%)
#40 -	20 (87%)*	1 (4%)	0 (0%)	3 (13%)	0 (0%)	0 (0%)
#41 -	2 (9%)	17 (74%)*	1 (4%)	3 (13%)	0 (0%)	0 (0%)
#42 -	2 (9%)	1 (4%)	18 (78%)*	2 (9%)	0 (0%)	0 (0%)

M1173 - 12: Organize and analyze data by applying statistical methods.
(S.8.B.4a, S.10.A.4a, S.10.B.4, S.10.C.4b)

Item	A	B	C	D	E	Space
#1 -	0 (0%)	18 (78%)*	5 (22%)	0 (0%)	0 (0%)	0 (0%)
#2 -	4 (17%)	0 (0%)	0 (0%)	19 (83%)*	0 (0%)	0 (0%)
#3 -	0 (0%)	2 (9%)	18 (78%)*	3 (13%)	0 (0%)	0 (0%)
#4 -	2 (9%)	17 (74%)*	3 (13%)	1 (4%)	0 (0%)	1 (4%)
#5 -	0 (0%)	3 (13%)	17 (74%)*	2 (9%)	0 (0%)	1 (4%)
#6 -	2 (9%)	1 (4%)	0 (0%)	19 (83%)*	0 (0%)	1 (4%)
#7 -	2 (9%)	2 (9%)	19 (83%)*	0 (0%)	0 (0%)	0 (0%)
#8 -	14 (61%)*	2 (9%)	3 (13%)	4 (17%)	0 (0%)	0 (0%)
#9 -	0 (0%)	2 (9%)	21 (91%)*	0 (0%)	0 (0%)	0 (0%)
#10 -	2 (9%)	4 (17%)	16 (70%)*	1 (4%)	0 (0%)	0 (0%)
#11 -	7 (30%)*	3 (13%)	1 (4%)	11 (48%)	0 (0%)	1 (4%)
#12 -	1 (4%)	3 (13%)	19 (83%)*	0 (0%)	0 (0%)	0 (0%)
#13 -	0 (0%)	0 (0%)	0 (0%)	23 (100%)*	0 (0%)	0 (0%)
#14 -	1 (4%)	20 (87%)*	2 (9%)	0 (0%)	0 (0%)	0 (0%)
#15 -	21 (91%)*	0 (0%)	2 (9%)	0 (0%)	0 (0%)	0 (0%)
#16 -	17 (74%)*	0 (0%)	1 (4%)	5 (22%)	0 (0%)	0 (0%)
#17 -	4 (17%)	13 (57%)*	4 (17%)	2 (9%)	0 (0%)	0 (0%)
#18 -	2 (9%)	1 (4%)	2 (9%)	18 (78%)*	0 (0%)	0 (0%)
#19 -	1 (4%)	14 (61%)*	5 (22%)	3 (13%)	0 (0%)	0 (0%)

(continued)

Table 5.4. (*continued*)

M1173 - 15: Apply geometric knowledge of polynomials including formulas for perimeter and area. (S.7.A.4a, S.9.B.4)

Item	A	B	C	D	E	Space
#52 -	22 (96%)*	1 (4%)	0 (0%)	0 (0%)	0 (0%)	0 (0%)
#53 -	2 (9%)	3 (13%)	7 (30%)	11 (48%)*	0 (0%)	0 (0%)
#54 -	0 (0%)	3 (13%)	18 (78%)*	2 (9%)	0 (0%)	0 (0%)
#55 -	3 (13%)	14 (61%)*	2 (9%)	4 (17%)	0 (0%)	0 (0%)
#56 -	2 (9%)	2 (9%)	2 (9%)	17 (74%)*	0 (0%)	0 (0%)
#57 -	0 (0%)	2 (9%)	21 (91%)*	0 (0%)	0 (0%)	0 (0%)
#58 -	14 (61%)*	1 (4%)	1 (4%)	7 (30%)	0 (0%)	0 (0%)
#59 -	1 (4%)	21 (91%)*	1 (4%)	0 (0%)	0 (0%)	0 (0%)
#60 -	15 (65%)*	3 (13%)	3 (13%)	2 (9%)	0 (0%)	0 (0%)
#61 -	3 (13%)	9 (39%)*	8 (35%)	3 (13%)	0 (0%)	0 (0%)
#62 -	2 (9%)	4 (17%)	17 (74%)*	0 (0%)	0 (0%)	0 (0%)
#63 -	13 (57%)*	3 (13%)	5 (22%)	1 (4%)	0 (0%)	1 (4%)
#64 -	0 (0%)	4 (17%)	9 (39%)	10 (43%)*	0 (0%)	0 (0%)
#65 -	4 (17%)	2 (9%)	16 (70%)*	1 (4%)	0 (0%)	0 (0%)
#66 -	6 (26%)	17 (74%)*	0 (0%)	0 (0%)	0 (0%)	0 (0%)
#67 -	4 (17%)	1 (4%)	18 (78%)*	0 (0%)	0 (0%)	0 (0%)
#68 -	7 (30%)	1 (4%)	0 (0%)	15 (65%)*	0 (0%)	0 (0%)
#69 -	12 (52%)*	10 (43%)	1 (4%)	0 (0%)	0 (0%)	0 (0%)
#70 -	3 (13%)	16 (70%)*	3 (13%)	1 (4%)	0 (0%)	0 (0%)
#71 -	6 (26%)	6 (26%)	8 (35%)*	3 (13%)	0 (0%)	0 (0%)

poorly on a particular objective, then the teacher may need to reteach the objective before moving on to new material. This report also points out particular questions that were difficult for students. For example, question 11 was correctly answered by only 30 percent, or seven of the twenty-three students. Is it a poorly written question? Was information presented that made 48 percent of the students believe D was the correct answer? These are questions the teacher needs to answer before the class moves on to the next unit.

An item analysis by objective report should be run for all grades or sections taking the test. Table 4.4 in chapter 4 is an example of an item analysis by objective report run for all 390 students taking a biology common assessment. This report is helpful in answering broader curriculum questions in that it shows how all students performed.

In this case, when a larger group of students fails to meet objectives, both the curriculum and the assessments need to be examined. Perhaps the textbook doesn't cover an objective adequately and additional materials need to be used. Perhaps more time needs to be allotted to teaching the objective, and/or perhaps the test questions have been written in a confusing or misleading manner and need to be revised. It often is useful to use the item analysis by objective report in combination with the standard mastery report, which shows which objectives students have mastered and which they have not (table 4.5).

These score reports work well for forced choice/multiple choice tests, such as the seventy-one-item test given to algebra students. However, it is also possible to score and receive item analyses for rubric-graded writing assignments, projects, labs, and speeches. In this case, the teacher reads the written project or listens to the speech or performance and then fills in the rubric, which has been aligned with the curriculum objectives.

Figure 5.1 is an example of an online speech rubric that was completed by a teacher using a laptop computer. Figure 5.2 is an example of a writing rubric that can be scanned after the teacher scores a writing assignment by completing a rubric for each student in a class or group of classes. In either case, after the class or group of students completes the performance and the teacher fills in the rubrics, the rubrics are scanned and scored, and the reports are requested. Both online testing and grading and the computerized scoring of rubrics greatly speed up the process of scoring and reporting student work. (See the online testing section in Key Resources.)

Even with writing assessments and speeches, it is helpful to see how students performed on the curriculum objectives. Table 5.5 shows how 470 students performed on the speech assessment. The criteria for the speech and the curriculum objectives for the course are summarized in the left column. The number and percentage of students "not meeting," "meeting," and "exceeding" the objectives/criteria are listed to the right.

2002/2003 Speech Local Assessment

Mrs. Thomas   INTRO SPEECH   Period | 4

SMITH, ERIC   2040115

Topic	Exceeds	Gestures	Meets
Attention-Getting Opening	Exceeds	Articulation	Exceeds
Preview	Exceeds	Rate of Speaking	Exceeds
Supporting Details	Exceeds	Fluency	Exceeds
Transitions Used	Meets	Volume	Meets
Main Points	Exceeds	Enthusiasm	Meets
Sequence	Exceeds	Supplemental	Meets
Topic Summary	Exceeds	Organization	Exceeds
Clincher	Exceeds		
Facial	Exceeds		
Eye Contact	Does Not Meet		
Posture	Exceeds		

Total: | 172

0 = Does Not Meet
7 = Meets
10 = Exceeds

Wednesday, October 01, 2003

Figure 5.1. *Individual Student Report for an Online Speech Rubric*
Source: DuPage High School District 88, 2003. Reprinted with permission.

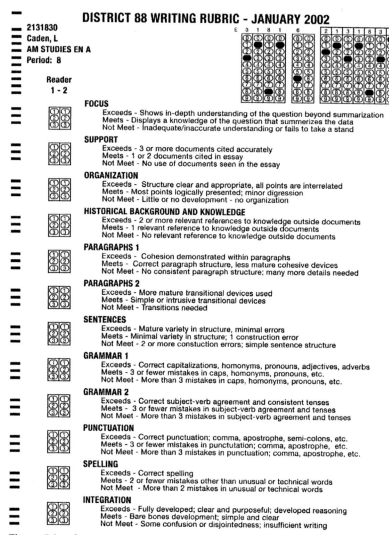

DISTRICT 88 WRITING RUBRIC - JANUARY 2002

2131830
Caden, L
AM STUDIES EN A
Period: 8

Reader
1 - 2

FOCUS
Exceeds - Shows in-depth understanding of the question beyond summarization
Meets - Displays a knowledge of the question that summarizes the data
Not Meet - Inadequate/inaccurate understanding or fails to take a stand

SUPPORT
Exceeds - 3 or more documents cited accurately
Meets - 1 or 2 documents cited in essay
Not Meet - No use of documents seen in the essay

ORGANIZATION
Exceeds - Structure clear and appropriate, all points are interrelated
Meets - Most points logically presented; minor digression
Not Meet - Little or no development - no organization

HISTORICAL BACKGROUND AND KNOWLEDGE
Exceeds - 2 or more relevant references to knowledge outside documents
Meets - 1 relevant reference to knowledge outside documents
Not Meet - No relevant reference to knowledge outside documents

PARAGRAPHS 1
Exceeds - Cohesion demonstrated within paragraphs
Meets - Correct paragraph structure, less mature cohesive devices
Not Meet - No consistent paragraph structure; many more details needed

PARAGRAPHS 2
Exceeds - More mature transitional devices used
Meets - Simple or intrusive transitional devices
Not Meet - Transitions needed

SENTENCES
Exceeds - Mature variety in structure, minimal errors
Meets - Minimal variety in structure; 1 construction error
Not Meet - 2 or more constuction errors; simple sentence structure

GRAMMAR 1
Exceeds - Correct capitalizations, homonyms, pronouns, adjectives, adverbs
Meets - 3 or fewer mistakes in caps, homonyms, pronouns, etc.
Not Meet - More than 3 mistakes in caps, homonyms, pronouns, etc.

GRAMMAR 2
Exceeds - Correct subject-verb agreement and consistent tenses
Meets - 3 or fewer mistakes in subject-verb agreement and tenses
Not Meet - More than 3 mistakes in subject-verb agreement and tenses

PUNCTUATION
Exceeds - Correct punctuation; comma, apostrophe, semi-colons, etc.
Meets - 3 or fewer mistakes in punctutation; comma, apostrophe, etc.
Not Meet - More than 3 mistakes in punctuation; comma, apostrophe, etc.

SPELLING
Exceeds - Correct spelling
Meets - 2 or fewer mistakes other than unusual or technical words
Not Meet - More than 2 mistakes in unusual or technical words

INTEGRATION
Exceeds - Fully developed; clear and purposeful; developed reasoning
Meets - Bare bones development; simple and clear
Not Meet - Some confusion or disjointedness; insufficient writing

Figure 5.2. Scanable Writing Rubric

The district writing assessment, given to all juniors, is scored by two teachers. Each teacher gives a score of 1, 2, or 3 to indicate if a student exceeds, meets, or does not meet the twelve scoring traits on the writing rubric.

Source: DuPage High School District 88, 2002. Reprinted with permission.

The results of this assessment indicate that teachers need to help students develop the body of their speeches with more supporting detail and use more eye contact when presenting their speeches. While these weaknesses would not be a surprise to any teacher who ever asked high school sophomores to present a speech, the report does objectively identify two major weakness and would argue for a teacher team or department chair or curriculum director to find resources to help remediate the weaknesses.

Table 5.5. Summary Report for Local Speech Assessment

After the district speech assessment was given to all sophomore speech students, the online scoring was summarized in the following report for 470 students:

Willowbrook High School 2002–2003 Speech Local Assessment

Topic	Not Meet		Meets		Exceeds	
Attention-Getting Opening	12	3%	37	8%	421	90%
Introduction-Preview	9	2%	167	36%	294	63%
Body-Supporting Detail	48	10%	193	41%	229	49%
Body-Transition	48	10%	193	41%	229	49%
Body-Main Points	16	3%	99	21%	355	75%
Body-Sequence	24	5%	217	46%	229	49%
Conclusion-Topic Summary	21	4%	229	49%	220	47%
Conclusion-Clincher	29	6%	322	69%	119	25%
Presentation-Facial	7	1%	236	50%	227	48%
Presentation-Eye Contact	42	9%	203	43%	225	48%
Presentation-Posture	10	2%	345	73%	115	24%
Presentation-Gestures	8	2%	372	79%	90	19%
Voice-Articulation	12	3%	292	62%	166	35%
Voice-Rate of Speaking	15	3%	138	29%	317	67%
Voice-Fluency	19	4%	350	74%	101	21%
Voice-Volume	9	2%	111	24%	350	74%
Voice-Emphasis/Enthusiasm	26	6%	240	51%	204	43%
Supplemental Materials	42	9%	167	36%	261	56%
Organization/Outline	28	6%	83	18%	359	76%
Overall	**436**	**4%**	**4285**	**46%**	**4678**	**50%**

Source: DuPage High School District 88, 2003. Reprinted with permission.

DISAGGREGATION OF DATA

Either the item analysis of test questions or the item analysis by objective report may be run for a specific group of students, grouped by gender, race, ethnicity, curriculum type, or income level if the group is coded on the student's answer sheet. This separation of test results by subgroup is called disaggregation.

Disaggregation of data allows teachers, administrators, and interested citizens to examine how various subgroups are progressing toward standards. Disaggregation helps find subgroups that may be experiencing difficulty with a particular curriculum objective or set of test questions. Without disaggregation, the subgroup experiencing difficulty may be hidden in the overall average score of the larger group. Because No Child Left Behind (NCLB) requires that all subgroups reach achievement standards, schools need to disaggregate data on formative assessments for learning to determine how students in different subgroups are progressing toward meeting and exceeding standards.

A recent study focusing on state test scores of Chicago Public School students revealed that 85.3 percent came from low-income families, 50.8 percent were African American, 36.1 percent were Latino, 9.6 percent were white/non-Latino, 3.3 percent were Asian American, and 14.3 percent had limited English proficiency. Students from low-income families, African American families, and Latino families did less well than other students on the state tests (Commercial Club of Chicago 2003, 6, 65).

The 2002 state test scores showed that 30 percent of the African American students met or exceeded standards in reading and 16 percent met or exceeded standards in math; 35 percent of Latino students met or exceeded standards in reading and 26 percent in math; 60 percent white/non-Latino met or exceeded in reading and 55 percent in math; and 57 percent of Asian American students met or exceeded standards in reading and 62 percent in math (Commercial Club of Chicago 2003, 65).

The same study went on to say that there was no credible evidence to support the notion that children from poor families or particular ethnic groups were on average less capable of learning than others and that good teaching and effective schools were the "most important factors in student learning" (Commercial Club of Chicago 2003, 2). The study stated that "data-driven decision making and strong internal accountability systems [were] core characteristics of high-performing schools and [were] all but unknown in poorly performing ones" (Commercial Club of Chicago 2003, 52).

The study supported the notion that both assessments for learning and assessments of learning were crucial to increasing achievement. "Teachers need better information about how students are doing while they are learning, as well as after the fact. Teacher teams and building administrators need better information, on a more timely basis about the progress of classroom and grade level groups throughout the course of the school year" (Commercial Club of Chicago 2003, 52).

This recommendation is crucial, since every student regardless of race, ethnicity, or economic status is expected to meet or exceed state standards by 2014. By analyzing disaggregated data of formative assessments, a school, a teacher team, or an individual teacher is able to help students in different subgroups remediate their weaknesses before students take the high-stakes summative state assessment required by NCLB.

SELECTING AND USING DATA

Because schools are flooded with data, national score reports, state score reports, and local score reports, it is important to decide which data are the most useful to teachers, principals, students, and parents.

Individual teachers need to see data that is going to improve their teaching and their students' learning. Therefore the data must be relevant to an individual teacher's students and curriculum, and it must be timely so that it can be used by the teacher to remedy student weaknesses. The item analysis by objective report for a class or multiple sections taught by the same teacher is helpful because it shows exactly how a given teacher's students are performing on the curriculum objectives and gives the teacher necessary and timely information for helping students improve.

Teachers are generally more interested in the results of their classroom assessments than the results of state and national tests because of the timeliness of the results and specific relevance of the results to what has been taught by the teacher. Teachers tend to want to know how their students are doing now on the local curriculum.

Teacher teams, department chairs, and principals are interested in the item analysis by objective report for all students at a given grade level or all students in a course because it shows how a given group of students is progressing toward the curriculum objectives and the state standards. This is the report that tells teacher teams if different materials or additional time are needed to augment work on a particular objective. It also may show that some test items are poorly written or confusing to students. It is the report to use to improve the curriculum, the materials, and the pacing of the curriculum in general. It also is the report to make certain that the test questions are clear.

For data to be meaningful to teacher teams, department chairs, and principals, there should be consistency in data over time. The test should remain consistent from year to year so that changes in the curriculum, materials, and instructional practices can be measured. If a new textbook is used because a teacher team believes it will improve student learning, a similar test needs to be used from one year to the next to see if learning has really improved. If the test is changed along with the textbook, it will be more difficult to gauge the impact of the new text on student learning.

Students and parents are interested in the achievement of the individual student. Thus the individual student report (figure 5.1) tells how a specific student did on an individual test and how this student is progressing toward the state standards or objectives. Figure 5.1 shows Eric and his parents that he is a very good speaker but could improve his performance by making better eye contact with his audience. It's likely that Eric's parents also have noticed this weakness at home and could encourage him to "look me in the eye when you are speaking to me."

All the above mentioned reports deal with student progress on a school's local common curriculum as measured by its formative common assessments for learning. Parents and school officials also are interested in how students compare to students in other schools in neighboring communities, as well as across the state, the country, and the world. For this reason it is important for schools to track selected, normed, summative assessments reported in national quartiles.

It is not unusual for a child to exceed in many curriculum categories on local assessments and then have the parent question if the curriculum is too easy. In this situation a normed, national, or state test is helpful to show that the local curriculum and assessments are rigorous and the child in question also is in the top quartile in the country on a normed national test.

A board of education or community group could ask a similar question regarding a group of students, questioning whether the graduating classes' superior performance on local tests was a indication that they would also excel in college or the world of work. Again, in this situation, a normed, national, or state assessment would show how a particular group of students compared to peers across the country.

ASSESSMENT CENTERS

The sample reports in this chapter are examples of data collection and analysis generated in a school assessment center containing a computer, a scanner, and the appropriate software for completing item analyses of both objective tests and assessments that were rubric graded. The assessment center was staffed by a trained clerical staff member who scanned and scored tests and generated reports requested by either a teacher, a teacher team, a department chair, or an administrator.

During local assessments, such as high school common final exams, teachers brought their students' answer sheets or the teacher-completed rubrics to the assessment center for scoring. Scanned and scored tests were returned to the teacher within twenty-four hours, complete with numeric score and a letter grade. Reports were generated after all students took a particular local assessment and were returned to teachers and administrators in a timely manner so that teachers could review and discuss the results and initiate changes in the curriculum and/or instruction as soon as possible.

When local assessments were not being given, the assessment center was used to generate data about student attendance, graduation rates, and student participation in extra curricular activities, as well as to scan and score student, teacher, and parent surveys. The assessment center also tracked and stored students' scores on summative assessments of learning, such as state tests, the ACT, and the SAT.

Because students, teachers, administrators, parents, and community members all want information about student achievement, it is important for schools and districts to begin developing assessment centers to collect and store student test data that is useful and accessible to all members of the school community. The data that are now required for federal and state reports are extremely helpful to the school improvement process and are complementary to the data collected from formative common local assessments. Thus if schools build an organized and efficient means of collecting, storing, and providing meaningful data, they will aid teachers in improving instruction and in remediating the weaknesses of their students; help students, teachers, parents, and administrators in evaluating students' progress toward standards; and provide access to the necessary information to report students' strengths and weaknesses to the community and to government agencies.

CHECKLIST FOR GATHERING MEANINGFUL DATA

	Not Yet	In Progress	Completed
1. Tests are analyzed to provide item analysis by objective and other reports that are useful in identifying and prioritizing goals to improve the curriculum, classroom achievement, and individual student achievement.	_____	_____	_____
2. Assessment data are provided to individual teachers, teacher teams, and administrators to make changes in instructional practices and curriculum in a timely manner.	_____	_____	_____
3. Test data have been disaggregated and results have been reviewed to identify and determine the needs of underachieving subgroups.	_____	_____	_____
4. Tests are consistent over time so that longitudinal data may be collected and reviewed over time.	_____	_____	_____
5. Local assessment data are compared with state and national data to ensure that local curriculum and instructional practices meet or exceed state and national standards.	_____	_____	_____

KEY RESOURCES

Assessment Software

Assessment analysis and data management and reporting are important to the process of using data to increase student achievement and to the demands of NCLB legislation. Some states offer schools software that aligns test items with state standards. However, a variety of commercial software products also enable schools to align assessments to state standards and generate student reports in relation to state standards. Many of these products also transfer standards and curriculum objectives directly to teachers' grade books and provide the means to chart progress of individual students, groups of students, classes, and schools. A summary of some of these products may be found at www.educational-software-directory.net/teacher's/assessment.html.

While most assessment software focuses on item analysis of forced choice tests, it is possible to use survey software to scan rubrics and produce reports tied to the primary scoring traits of a rubric.

Online Testing

Schools are encouraged to use their computer labs and laptop resources for online testing. A teacher with a laptop can input student data into an online rubric. As the student is giving a speech or completing a lab experiment, the teacher inputs data for each student into the online rubric. After data for all students are entered, reports can be produced that analyze the strengths and weaknesses of all the teacher's students based on the criteria set forth in the rubric. (See table 5.5.)

Several textbook publishers offer test packages that are aligned with the text and that can be placed online and aligned with standards. The content and format of the test items mirror the state standards tests. Score reports are designed to reflect students' progress toward state standards.

There also is commercial software that aligns pools or banks of online test questions to state standards. Questions can be randomly drawn from test question banks and scrambled to provide test variety. Schools can assign a passing score and a time limit for the test. Students take tests in the school's computer lab during a class or at another time. Once the test is taken, it can be scored immediately, and group reports can be printed after an entire class or group of students has completed the assessment.

CHAPTER 6

Using Assessment Data
to Increase Student Achievement

Once data have been collected and analyzed, methods to remediate students' weaknesses and build on their strengths need to be explored and developed. With item analyses of test results tied to standards, teachers and administrators will have powerful information to help students and raise achievement to meet or exceed state standards.

Unless data are collected and analyzed, improvement does not occur on a regular basis. In most schools students take tests; however, teachers and administrators do not always take the time to look at the results of local tests to consider what students have learned and what they still need to work on. As Wiggins (1993) points out, "It is rare for schools to collect and analyze exemplary student work and teacher-graded work to ensure that standards are clear and held in common. It is equally rare to see the analysis of student performance errors as a regular item for faculty meeting discussion" (279). Yet meaningful change and improvement in student learning and achievement take place through the analysis of student work.

Once the test results are analyzed, the changes that will lead to improvement will fall into four basic categories: curriculum and assessment revision, data-driven classroom instruction, individual student remediation, and staff development. While these categories focus on different types of efforts, they all begin with people looking at data, identifying areas of weakness, and determining remedies for the weaknesses. This is an important process and needs to be given time and attention by teachers and administrators.

CURRICULUM AND ASSESSMENT REVISION

The change process falls into a continuum. At one end are large-scale changes that affect all students. At the other end are small-scale changes or methods of individual help that only affect a few students. Changing the curriculum is a large-scale change that is an effective means for improving the achievement of many students.

In 2004 math scores on the Illinois Standards Achievement Test at Chicago's Little Village Elementary School jumped from 43 percent to 92 percent meeting standards in third grade and from 34 percent to 68 percent meeting standards in fifth grade. The school attributes this improvement to the adoption of a new math curriculum that emphasizes higher-order thinking and hands-on training for teachers (Dell'Angela 2004).

In addition to changing the curriculum, it is crucial to examine timing and pacing. Students frequently do poorly on a test because a subject or topic has not been adequately covered in the curriculum prior to their taking the state test. Perhaps the topic is not included in the curriculum, such as the earth science example discussed in chapter 3; or perhaps the topic is in the curriculum but is not studied in depth and sufficiently covered in the textbook or with supplementary materials. (See textbooks aligned with state standards in the Key Resources section at the end of the chapter.) Or perhaps the topic is covered in the curriculum after the students take the local assessment or state test. Any of these problems is easily remedied by adjusting the curriculum and adding new instructional materials and formative assessments to address the topic before students take the state's summative test.

Schools also must ascertain that the majority of students have exposure to the curriculum standards that are tested by the state. A school may align the local curriculum with state standards but not have graduation requirements that ensure all students have exposure to the state standards. For example, most states have math standards that require knowledge of algebra and geometry. Yet in many high schools the math graduation requirement may be fulfilled by taking prealgebra and algebra, causing large numbers of students to have no exposure to geometry. Because the state test requires knowledge of algebra and geometry, schools in this situation need to revamp their graduation requirements as well as the math curriculum so that all students are exposed to algebra and geometry before taking the state test as juniors.

Though schools in this situation often consider adding geometry as a third required year of math, they discover that adding more yearly requirements isn't a good solution because there isn't enough time in students' schedules to continually add requirements. Rather, it is better to examine course sequences and vertical alignment to make certain that standards are met by existing requirements prior to the state testing of juniors. As already noted, test results improve dramatically once students are taught the material.

DATA-DRIVEN CLASSROOM INSTRUCTION

Another way to increase student achievement is for teachers to use the data to change instruction. While this method will not have the large-scale effect that changing the curriculum and materials has, it will improve achievement for most students in an individual teacher's classroom. If individual teachers review item analyses by objective for their individual classes, they will quickly see that their students perform well on some objectives but not others.

Table 4.5 (in chapter 4) is an example of a standard mastery report for biology. The report shows that 24 percent of the students did not meet the local assessment standards for cell physiology. This is important information for the biology teacher and should signal the need to go back and reteach key topics in cell physiology. A good teacher will not only reteach the topic but will use new methods and approaches.

Often a topic needs to be broken down into smaller steps in order for students to master it. For example, it is not unusual for students to have difficulty answering specific questions about a broad concept, such as the scientific method. Though students are able to complete lab experiments and the related lab write-ups, they have trouble distinguishing the parts of the scientific method (define the problem, collect information, form a hypothesis, observe and record data, and draw a conclusion) from one another.

To individualize help for these students, good teachers develop rubrics to help students distinguish the parts of a large concept. Some science teachers use a teaching method known as clipboard cruising (Graham 1998). On their clipboard is a chart or rubric containing student names and the different components of the scientific method. As students are completing lab experiments, the teacher "cruises" around to students' lab stations and questions students about their hypothesis, their data, and their conclusion. The students who can easily distinguish between the parts of the scientific method receive clipboard checks, signifying their understanding of the components.

For students struggling with the identification of the components, the clipboard cruise creates a teachable moment for the teacher to reteach the scientific method by breaking down the concept into smaller parts. Stopping at the lab station, the teacher can discuss the components of the scientific method with the student, help the student break down the components in a lab application setting, and, after discussion, check for student understanding.

Teachers also may reteach a concept by focusing on a different student learning style. The teaching of elementary reading most often is initiated using phonics, which addresses an auditory learning style. However, teachers frequently help struggling students by using a different learning style to reteach a sound. For example, in reteaching, students may be asked to trace a sound in a shallow box of sand and thus use their tactile senses to better understand the concept, or they may be asked to associate a new sound, such as B, with a picture of a bee, thus accessing their visual senses to learn the new concept.

Reteaching is an important step in changing the achievement level of a class, but arguments against it will be raised by the very teachers who need to do it. The most common argument is that there is no time to reteach. Many teachers believe they must continue to move through the curriculum and cover the material even when students have not learned the basics. They say that they cannot take the time to reteach material not understood by their students because they must move on to the remaining material in the curriculum.

A crowded curriculum is a common problem and is one of the strongest arguments for examining the curriculum in order to remove extraneous or redundant material and create more time to reteach material that has not been understood by students.

In some high schools only a small percentage of students meets state standards. Yet, regardless of the low scores, there is resistance from teachers who claim they cannot/will not align their local curriculum with the state standards because if they covered all the basic material required by the state, they would not have time to teach the concepts necessary for students to be successful in college.

Almost every school has teachers who believe their personal standards are higher and inherently better than the state or national standards. These teachers need to be reminded that it is their responsibility to help all students meet or exceed state standards, and it is the role of upper-level, capstone courses and AP courses to prepare students for college.

The reluctance to reteach may also be a sign that the teacher needs additional methods training in a particular subject. For many years colleges and universities were sending English majors off to teach English with little training in how to teach writing. Most English teachers were literature majors and took few writing courses and no methods courses in how to teach writing. They would assign a topic (e.g., What did you do on your summer vacation?) and a length, two pages, and that would be it. It was not until research had been completed on the writing process and teachers were taught how people actually learned to write that teachers were able to break down a writing assignment into teachable segments, such as prewriting, outlining, drafting, and revising, and help students understand and use the writing process.

The need to reteach parts of the curriculum with more effective instructional methods may be a signal for additional staff development to help retrain teachers to teach or reteach segments of curriculum content more effectively. In addition to teacher retraining workshops and graduate courses, many new teaching strategies may be found on the Internet. (See state assessment websites in the Key Resources section.)

The Region 10 Educational Service Center in Texas offers sample tests that are aligned with the State of Texas Assessment of Academic Skills and Texas curriculum objectives. Teachers may access a website that shows test questions and an analysis of responses (figure 6.1). By clicking on the wrong answer, the teacher receives a brief analysis of what a student may have been thinking when selecting the response (figure 6.2). By clicking on the correct answer, the teacher receives teaching strategies and activities to prepare students to better understand the question and the curriculum objective (figure 6.3).

Figure 6.1 is an example of a seventh-grade math question on graphing, where students are asked to study a graph and select the response that is most accurately represented by the graph. Figure 6.2 is an example of the wrong answer and explains to the teacher that the student did not understand that the graph was in multiples of two, indicating a rate change of $2.00. Figure 6.3 gives the teacher a series of exercises for teaching or reteaching students to better understand concepts behind the graphing of multiples.

Sample Math Question from State of Texas Test

1. The graph shows the cost of buying tickets to an intramural basketball game.

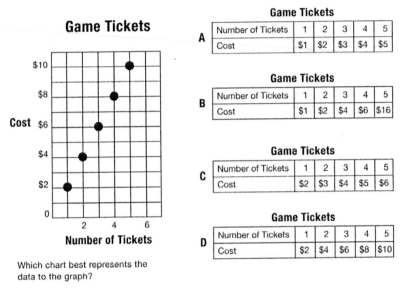

Game Tickets

A

Number of Tickets	1	2	3	4	5
Cost	$1	$2	$3	$4	$5

Game Tickets

B

Number of Tickets	1	2	3	4	5
Cost	$1	$2	$4	$6	$16

Game Tickets

C

Number of Tickets	1	2	3	4	5
Cost	$2	$3	$4	$5	$6

Game Tickets

D

Number of Tickets	1	2	3	4	5
Cost	$2	$4	$6	$8	$10

Which chart best represents the data to the graph?

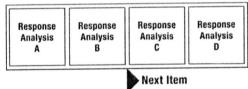

Response Analysis A	Response Analysis B	Response Analysis C	Response Analysis D

▶ **Next Item**

Figure 6.1. Sample Question from State of Texas Test

Source: Region 10 Educational Service Center, Texas, 2000, *TAAS Mathematics*, www.ednet10 .net/taas/s00/go7/i01/q.html (accessed March 2004).

Explanation of Incorrect Response B

This response choice is a table that pairs the number of tickets bought (1–5) to the corresponding costs, $1 to $16. The given graph indicates that each ticket cost $2, but the table begins with 1 ticket costing $1, then simply pairs each new amount of tickets with a cost that equals the preceding cost doubled. For example, 3 tickets cost $4, so 4 tickets cost $8. Students did not know that the ordered pairs of the points on the graph failed to match the corresponding pairs in the table.

Click on the correct response choice, D, for suggested instructional activities.

Response Choice Selection:
(<u>A</u>) B (<u>C</u>) (<u>D</u>)

Back To Test Item Content
Return To Test Item Selection

Figure 6.2. Sample Incorrect Response: State of Texas Test

Source: Region 10 Educational Service Center, Texas, 2000, *TAAS Mathematics*, www.ednet10
.net/taas/s00/go7/i01/a.html (accessed March 2004).

Sample Instructional Activities

Many students have difficulty locating points on grids for given ordered pairs and vice versa. For this test item involving a scatter plot (a set of disconnected points on a grid), students had to recognize ordered pairs in both graphic and tabular format. The following activities will provide them with experiences in translating tables of values to grid points for either scatter plots or line graphs.

(1) Manipulative Stage:

This activity may be done with the class as a whole. Count off 8 students in order from one or two rows where they are sitting. Give each numbered student about 30 one-inch square tiles or paper squares. Draw a line segment near the lower edge of the chalkboard to represent the horizontal axis of the graph and mark off this axis approximately in 2-inch intervals. Label the marks left to right from 1 to 8. Draw a 2-column table on the board to the side of the horizontal axis. Title the left column as "Student Position" and the right column as "Total Tiles." Now select students 1, 2, 3, 4, and 5 from the original 8 students, and record their positions 1–5 in the left column of the table. Have the five students take to the board the amount of tiles or paper squares that equals their own position's multiple of 3; for example, student 1 takes 3 tiles, student 2 takes 6 tiles, etc. Record these amounts in the right column of the table. Tape each student's tiles in a column one tile wide above that student's position number on the axis. The finished graph will look like an increasing vertical bar graph made of tiles. Now draw a large dot on the board at the center of the top edge of each column of tiles. The large dots now represent a scatter plot. To develop a line graph, add colored yarn as follows. Connecting from left to right, tape a long piece of colored yarn to the board at each of the large dots to create the appearance of a line segment. Cut the excess yarn off at the first and last dots; do not connect from those two dots back down to the drawn horizontal axis. (This class graph will be used for the activity at the Pictorial Stage that follows.)

Sample of the columns of tiles:

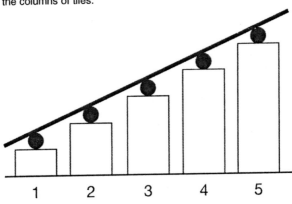

Figure 6.3a.

After students have transferred the above tile graph to grid paper (described in the Pictorial Stage), repeat the activity, using student 2, student 5, student 6, and student 8 with their multiples of 3: 6, 15, 18, and 24. Record the amounts in their proper columns in a new table on the board. Remind those students building the tile columns that they must first locate their position number on the horizontal axis, then build a column of tiles as tall as their assigned multiple. Relate these two actions to the corresponding numbers in the table. This activity may also be repeated, using multiples of 2 or multiples of 4, as well as a new group of 8 students.

(2) Pictorial Stage:

Now give each student a sheet of centimeter grid paper and a red pencil. A tile line graph from the Manipulative Stage should still be on the board. Use the longer edge of the grid paper for the vertical axis. Have students label the left vertical axis of their grids in unit intervals and label the axis as "Total Tiles." The lower horizontal axis should show the numbers 1 through 8 and be labeled "Student Position." Now have students represent the large dots of the tile line graph on their own grids and connect these new dots by drawing a straight red path between adjacent dots. (For a scatter plot, do not draw the red path to connect the dots.) The dots on the grid should represent the same vertical distance as the top edges of the tile columns. That is, if 6 tiles were used to make a column on the board, then the column's dot should match to a dot on the grid that is 6 units up from the horizontal axis. Also have students draw the tile line graph's corresponding table of values in the upper right corner of their grid paper. Prepare a new grid and table of values for each tile line graph made at the previous stage. For varied practice, make a horizontal table of values instead of the two-column vertical table described earlier.

Here is an incomplete drawing of the graph that corresponds to the first example discussed in the Manipulative Stage:

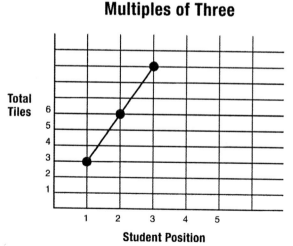

Multiples of Three

Figure 6.3b.

After students have completed their various line graphs (or scatter plots), ask them questions about each graph. Here are some higher level questions about the first graph, "Multiples of Three," that require students to compute with values from the graph:

How many students had more than 6 tiles in the columns they built? (3)

How many students helped build this tile line graph? (5)

How many tiles did student 2 and student 5 use in all for their two columns together? (21)

Response Choice Selection:
(A) (B) (C) D

Back To Test Item Content
Return To Test Item Selection

Figure 6.3. **Sample Instructional Activities: State of Texas Test**

Source: From Region 10 Educational Service Center, Texas, 2000, *TAAS Mathematics*, www.ednet10
.net/taas/s00/go7/i01/d.html (accessed March 2004).

INDIVIDUAL STUDENT REMEDIATION

At the small-scale end of the continuum are the various means for helping individual students achieve at a higher level. Item analyses of formative assessments identify a student's gaps in understanding and provide teachers with ample information to help a child remediate weaknesses before a high-stakes state or national exam. The challenge is for schools to have a system in place to help individual students remediate their weaknesses and not have the help for individual students fall solely on the shoulders of the student's teacher. Schools need a system for offering help to individual students and a common commitment from administrators, teachers, and support staff that all students will be helped to reach the curriculum standards.

There are three basic steps for establishing a system for helping individual students.

1. Use test data to identify students' individual strengths and weaknesses. The referral to any program to help students should be based on student data that provides accurate information about a student's strengths and weaknesses and, when necessary, the causes of the student's learning problems. Data from formative assessments provide this information and help determine whether the student needs one or two sessions with a tutor on the causes of the Civil War or needs to be enrolled in a semester of developmental reading.

Referrals need to be initiated by the student's teacher and transferred to the individual who has the power and capacity to select the appropriate help program in a timely manner. In most schools, this person is a guidance counselor. Unless there is a designated contact, a remediation program may falter in providing appropriate and timely help to the student.

2. Develop a sequential system for helping students remediate their weaknesses. Teachers, counselors, and social workers need to suggest student help programs that progress from voluntary and unstructured to being required and structured. Good communication should inform all teachers, parents, students, and counselors about the programs in the system and the means for referring students to the appropriate level of help.

To increase the achievement on an individual basis, many students only need a few extra minutes of individual help from their teacher. Certainly person-to-person contact and a positive student-teacher relationship is an ideal and economical way to increase achievement. Unfortunately, this type of help may place a huge burden on an individual teacher, who may have too many students to help in this manner.

In large high schools, where many teachers have 150 or more students, an instructional resource center is a good solution to helping students on an individual basis. Students can meet one-on-one with teachers and tutors to receive individual help. This type of resource is an example of a help program that is at the unstructured and optional end of the continuum: students voluntarily go to the IRC (instructional resources center) to receive help during study hall or before or after school.

The continuum becomes more structured and less voluntary when students are assigned to the IRC on contract for a semester. Students have to report five times a week for help until their classroom teacher and counselor decide the weaknesses are remediated and extra help is no longer needed (DuPage High School District 88).

A number of schools also have student writing labs, where a student may receive help from a teacher assigned to the writing lab or student tutor on a writing assignment. Another option is a guided study hall, where the study hall teacher has been advised by the classroom teacher of a student's missing assignments and makes certain the student completes the assignments in a timely manner.

If students' weaknesses do not respond to less structured, voluntary help measures, then more highly structured programs need to provide help. Frequently, students who do not respond to the voluntary forms of help have a long-term deficiency, such as poor reading skills, and may need special summer programs or an additional reading class that will improve their reading skills. A number of schools examine students' entry level reading and math scores and recommend or require summer school programs for students who are below grade-level performance in these areas.

Finally, poor academic performance may also be triggered by family or emotional problems, substance abuse, or other problems that may require attendance in a support group or intensive counseling.

3. Monitor student progress. Once a student is receiving extra help, progress should be regularly monitored to determine if the weaknesses are being remediated or if another form of help is needed.

Once a student's weaknesses have been identified through test analysis, a process of remediation of those weaknesses should begin as soon as possible. The key to helping an individual student improve is a wide and well-publicized continuum of help for the student, a continuum that begins with a program that is optional and less structured and progresses to programs that are mandatory and more tightly structured. The help is publicized in that teachers, parents, and students know these help programs are available to students and know how to access the continuum of help. Most schools have help programs. Unfortunately, they often are well-kept secrets.

Many schools are using technology to improve the communication process among students, teachers, and parents. School websites that outline class projects and homework assignments help students, parents, and tutors in understanding expectations and assignments. (See school website development in the Key Resources section.)

A number of schools are using online grading systems to improve both internal and external communications. The school's website allows teachers, students, and parents to access grades in progress and attendance from any computer with an Internet connection. (See online grades in Key Resources.)

Voice mail messaging systems also are an effective means to communicate daily homework assignments. (See voice messaging systems in Key Resources.) If a student is ill or a parent is wondering if there really is "no homework," all they have to do is phone a number, punch in the teacher's code, and listen to the teacher explain the homework assignment.

This type of voice messaging system is helpful to tutors in the previously discussed IRC example. A tutor calls into the system to listen to the teacher describe an assignment or series of assignments and then helps the student understand and complete the assignment. Of course, if the tutor has additional questions about the assignment or the student's weaknesses, the tutor contacts the classroom teacher directly.

STAFF DEVELOPMENT

If schools are going to use data to improve student achievement, regular time needs to be allotted for teachers to meet, review the data, and collaborate regarding changes in curriculum and instructional methods. Clearly one of the most meaningful methods of staff development is for a team of teachers to review the item analysis for a recent assessment and discuss areas of strength and weakness in students' progress toward the standards. These meetings foster change in curriculum as teachers "share the wealth" of what worked for them and learn new strategies from their colleagues. Teachers report that when they review data in team meetings, their instruction becomes more focused on standards and more goal oriented toward helping students meet or exceed standards.

In addition to changes in textbooks and materials, team meetings also foster changes in pacing and methodology. When team meetings focus on pacing, the team will learn that one teacher may go into great depth on many of the standards but have trouble covering all the material by the end of the year. Another teacher may move through the curriculum more rapidly but in less depth. As the discussion ensues, both teachers will be looking for ways their pacing can increase student achievement. The "in-depth" teacher may decide she spends too much time on a particular topic or a standard that isn't stressed on the state test. The "rapid" teacher may decide his students would perform better in all areas if he went into greater depth on each standard. The result of the team meeting should be that both teachers change the pacing of their instruction in ways the team believes will lead to increased student achievement in both teachers' classes.

In 2004 the state of Illinois initiated Academic Improvement Awards to honor schools with substantial gains in performance on the state tests over three years. In speaking to the principals of the award-winning schools, State Superintendent Robert Schiller reported key factors in school improvement that were reported in the principals' survey:

1. Nearly every principal cited strenuous efforts to align curriculum across grades with the Illinois learning standards.
2. Teamwork was not a buzzword for these schools; it required constant coaching, training, and collaboration building.
3. School teams studied test results and wrote action plans to improve both teaching and learning.
4. Improving test scores was only part of the challenge; the other part was changing attitudes toward change (Northern Illinois University 2004).

Team discussions can also supply recommendations for staff development workshops in curriculum areas where teachers need to learn new methodologies or materials. If DNA and cell physiology is introduced into the curriculum and the biology teachers did not study it in college, then they must be retooled so that they can show their students how to understand a DNA helix.

Finding time for team meetings is a challenge for every school. Yet, combined with data analysis, it is the most powerful method of staff development for increasing student achievement. Most schools have "institute days" and staff development time already integrated into their school calendars. Often this time is used for listening to a motivational speaker on an educational topic or visiting a local museum. While these activities may be entertaining to teachers, they do not come close to having the effect on student achievement that teacher team meetings do.

Steps for developing effective school improvement teams may be summarized as follows:

1. Teachers should be organized into teams according to grade level and/or subject area. In a grade school setting all fifth-grade teachers would be given time to meet to discuss their common curriculum and the results of common fifth-grade assessments. In a high school setting teams would be organized according to courses taught. All algebra teachers would be on one team; geometry teachers would be on another. In a large high school setting one teacher is likely to be on more than one team because they are likely to have more than one teaching prep. In a small high school, a team might be composed of the entire math department because there are not multiple teachers teaching a particular course. Rather, one teacher teaches all the sections of algebra, and another teaches all the sections of geometry.

Depending on the size of the school, teams should fall into different but logical patterns of membership. However, no matter how large or small the school, teams should be formed and have the opportunity to meet to examine data.

2. Teams should have time to meet on a regular basis. Again there is no predetermined formula for how often a team should meet. Meeting time depends on the structure of the school's schedule and calendar and the state of the curriculum and assessments when teams are formed. Many elementary schools are able to schedule weekly team meetings, whereas high schools may hold after-school team meetings on a monthly basis.

The number or frequency of meetings is not as important as the fact that teachers should have enough time, at least one hour, to review data and develop next steps. Summer is an excellent time for scheduling team meetings to address large curriculum and assessment projects.

3. Productive team meetings begin by focusing on data. The results of a common local assessment at any grade level for any subject will generate discussion on the need for curriculum revision, changes in instruction, changes in teaching materials, changes to the assessment, staff development needs, student remediation and support needs, and more. However, the meetings must begin with data.

4. All meetings should have a simple agenda. Because meeting time is precious, it is important to have an agenda to focus the discussion as well as to alert teachers regarding the materials they should bring to the team meeting. While individual teams may comfortably progress from meeting to meeting with a general knowledge of what the agenda will be, agendas greatly increase productivity for vertical team meetings, where fifth-, sixth-, and seventh-grade teams meet to discuss the sequence of fifth-, sixth-, and seventh-grade standards in science, or cross-departmental team meetings, such as when U.S. history teams meet with American literature teams to discuss how and when the standards regarding post–World War I American culture are being addressed by each subject.

5. An important part of every team meeting is the expectation of an outcome or action plan that will stimulate an improvement in student achievement. Teams need to do much more than look at the data. If improvement in learning is going to occur, then a change needs to be made in the system that produces the learning. An important part of every agenda is the expectation of an outcome that will stimulate an improvement in student achievement. Some schools address this change under the heading of curriculum or assessment revision. Other schools write goals. Others write goals and action plans. The format is not crucial. Building a culture of using data to foster continuous improvement in teaching and learning is.

If teachers are given time to analyze student achievement data, they will find new methods for improving the curriculum and new instructional methods for raising student achievement. By using data to monitor the effectiveness of their teaching strategies and by updating their repertoire of teaching strategies through carefully selected professional development opportunities, they will improve their effectiveness in the classroom and their students will achieve at a higher level. Most importantly, school leaders must nurture an attitude that data analysis is important and that teachers should have the time and skills to use it to foster continuous improvement in student achievement.

CHECKLIST FOR EFFECTIVE TEAM MEETINGS

	Not Yet	In Progress	Completed
1. Teacher teams have been organized by grade level and/or course.	____	____	____
2. Teacher teams have a regularly scheduled time to meet.	____	____	____
3. Teacher teams are provided with relevant, timely data regarding student achievement.	____	____	____
4. Teacher team meetings follow an agenda.	____	____	____
5. Teacher team meetings result in the identifying individual and programmatic changes and action plans to increase student achievement.	____	____	____

KEY RESOURCES

Textbooks Aligned with State Standards

One way to ensure the curriculum is addressing state standards is to select textbooks that are aligned with state standards. The major textbook companies have websites where teachers, textbook committees, and administrators can check the alignment of a potential textbook with state standards before the textbook is adopted by the school or district.

Schools are encouraged to go to the publisher's website, click on the alignment option, and review the textbook's alignment with the appropriate state standards. In most cases, a chart appears where the state standard is listed in a column on the left, and then chapters and exercises are listed left to right across the page, indicating where the standard is "introduced," "practiced," and "taught to mastery."

State Assessment Websites

Many states maintain assessment websites that have resources for students and teachers. Some states publish old state tests, enabling teachers to see the types and difficulty of questions on the state tests. Also, many states publish performance indicators that specify what students should know and be able to do at each grade level.

In addition, some sites have links to computerized tutorial programs containing questions aligned with state standards. Many teachers use these programs to help students remediate deficiencies in targeted areas. These programs contain diagnostic components, are flexible in that students work on areas that their teachers prescribe, and provide immediate feedback for both correct and incorrect answers. Teachers recommend that students work on programs in pairs and meet with the teacher after each tutorial session to discuss what they have learned and what they still have questions about.

School Websites

Numerous website solutions are available for schools. Some states offer schools free website software, but schools can also purchase website software in modules and thus add to their website as need and finances dictate. In addition to purchasing the website modules, schools can purchase services in the areas of design, training, and custom programming. Before launching a school website, schools are strongly encouraged to explore the legal responsibilities of maintaining a website. Copyright and student privacy issues are of extreme importance.

Online Grades

When teachers are provided with electronic grade books and attendance systems, paperwork decreases and communication increases. Keeping grades and attendance online gives students and parents the ability to access homework assignments, track grades and credits as they are in progress, and find valuable information regarding student attendance. E-mail components also may be added to web-based systems, further enhancing communication between home and school.

Voice Messaging Systems

A number of telephone companies offer voice messaging systems. The application in a school setting is that each teacher is given a voice mail box. The greeting records the teacher's message, which can be information about weekly assignments or deadlines for a large unit project. After parents or students call into the system, they dial in the teacher's mailbox code or extension number and then hear the teacher's message.

Most systems also allow a student or a parent to leave a message for the teacher, but this option may not be practical as the teacher may only want to access the system on a weekly basis to update assignments. Voice message systems increase communication between the school and the student or parent because school assignments can be accessed by phone from almost anywhere, twenty-four hours a day, seven days a week.

CHAPTER 7

Nurturing a Culture of
Accountability and Achievement

Building a thoughtful, rigorous common curriculum and developing common assessments that ask students to apply and interpret what they have learned in a meaningful way takes time and persistence. Though the process is not linear, following the stages of development suggested in the previous chapters is helpful. Begin by looking at the state standards. Then align the local curriculum to the standards, align the local assessments to the local curriculum, analyze the local assessment results, and study and act on the data.

When aligning the curriculum and assessments to standards, begin with the ones that have the greatest impact on students. At the high school level, this means beginning with freshman English, algebra, and U.S. history, the courses most students take, rather than singleton senior electives such as creative writing and advanced auto shop. At the elementary level, schools should begin with the grade levels and the subjects that will be tested by the state and then proceed with vertical articulation in those subjects, usually reading and math.

Don't expect all teachers to jump into the data-driven curriculum and assessment process with great enthusiasm. Many teachers don't support No Child Left Behind (NCLB) and are skeptical about the value of accountability and trying to objectively measure the learning that takes place in their classrooms. In addition, there are the general problems associated with asking any individual or system to change. For most people, change is uncomfortable and threatening. Remember that change happens in increments.

While NCLB will no doubt go through numerous changes, NCLB and standards-based education are not likely to go away. Most states either have standards or are adopting them, and states that have been implementing standards-based education for a number of years are beginning to see improvement. A case study of fifteen diverse school districts reflecting the status of NCLB implementation at the end of 2002–2003 found that school officials were "supportive of the general intent of NCLB to raise achievement for all students" and most were "hopeful their district [would] be able to achieve [the] goals" (Pinkerton, Kober, Scott, and Buell 2003, 2).

For schools to successfully implement NCLB and see improvement in student learning and achievement, change needs to occur. Though federal law requires schools to implement NCLB requirements, it is helpful for school leaders to remember that a standards-based curriculum, instruction, and assessment model requires teachers to work differently than they have in the past:

1. Teachers will be asked to teach differently than they were taught and to be accountable for student learning rather than just teaching. Rather than merely covering the curriculum, even a standards-based curriculum, teachers will need to assess what students have learned and decide whether or not it's time to move on to new material or go back and reteach topics students have not learned. Standards-based, data-driven instruction requires teaching lessons that are both measurable and consistently measured.

Effective teachers will need to plan to teach differently depending on the skill levels of their students. They will review, reteach, or adjust the pace of instruction based on their assessment of student learning. The pace at which instruction proceeds is one of the major reasons for ongoing teacher assessment of students.

2. Teachers also will be told what to teach. The teaching profession is filled with caring, creative individuals, many of whom have a large repertoire of engaging, carefully planned lessons. The challenge now is that a shift must occur to align these lessons with the standards. The major benefit of the standards to teachers and students is the focus they provide to teaching, learning, and assessment.

3. *Teachers will be asked to share their ideas and the results of their teaching, rather than work in isolation behind closed doors.* Teachers will be asked to join teams to review analyzed test data. As a result, they will see the strengths and weaknesses in their teaching, their students' learning, their curriculum, and their assessments. Rather than just moving on to the next unit of instruction, they must work with their colleagues to build on the strengths and make changes to remediate the weaknesses of their teaching as well as their students' learning.

A mature model for schools to consider is the College Board Advanced Placement Program. In existence for many years, the program has a standardized curriculum and common assessments, which students across the country take. The program holds schools, teachers, and students accountable for a rigorous curriculum and thoughtful, challenging common assessments. Students are rewarded, based on their test scores, with college credit, and teachers meet to review the results of their teaching and improve their curricular and instructional skills in highly regarded summer workshops.

Though change is difficult, if schools proceed through this process in a steady and consistent manner, change will occur. Once the process has begun, teachers will value team meetings and see the value of a standards-based curriculum. Initially annoyed at being told what to teach, most teachers eventually agree that the state standards are challenging, worthwhile curricular goals.

Though anxiety is associated with the state tests, especially for teachers whose grade levels and subject areas are being tested, the initial concerns centering on "teaching to the test" will subside. Schools need to make it clear, however, that no one is asking teachers to just "teach to the test" and certainly not to "teach the test," but rather teach a standards-based curriculum that will be tested. (See teaching to the test in the Key Resources section at the end of this chapter.)

Because the goal of a standards-based curriculum and assessment program is to improve learning by defining what students need to know and be able to do, the sharpened focus changes what and how teachers teach. When standards, local curriculum, and local assessments are aligned, "teaching to the test" becomes synonymous with teaching what students need to know and be able to do.

Once teachers audit the local curriculum in light of state standards and make appropriate adjustments to eliminate curricular redundancies and gaps, they will have written a local, standards-based curriculum that they can embrace. Similarly, once the local assessments are written to align with the curriculum and standards and include a variety of formats that are challenging to students and encourage higher-order thinking skills, teachers will own the local assessments and find that useful data can be extracted from these assessments to be used by teacher teams to diagnose areas where students are weak and define areas for curriculum revision and reteaching.

After the local curriculum and major common assessments are aligned to standards, a gradual shift in teachers' thinking will occur that will argue for quizzes and unit tests to become assessments for learning rather than assessment of learning. As teachers progress week to week through the curriculum, they will want to know what their students are learning and what they are not learning. With time, the teachers and students themselves will become hungry for data as well as knowledgeable consumers of data. Initially, only quarterly or semester tests will be standards-based formative assessments and subject to item analysis. However, with the use of test item banks and easy access to assessment centers, teachers will eventually transform more of their daily quizzes and unit tests to standards-based formative assessments for learning.

Each lesson, in a sense, will be viewed as a microcosm or piece of the entire curriculum. Good teachers will begin to look at each lesson and ask the following questions: What do I want students to know? How will I know if they know it? What will I do if they don't? They will view each lesson as a segment of the standards-based curriculum, and assessment of student learning will go much deeper than the yearly state summative assessment or a high school final exam that is subjected to item analysis. Teachers' assessment strategies will include quizzes and unit tests as well as students' responses to questions, students' body language, and students' participation in learning activities. Assessment will include all the formal and informal actions teachers take to monitor the learning of all students.

Teachers who are effective will learn to attend to the behaviors of all students. They will position themselves in classrooms and science labs so they can circulate around the room and not become absorbed with one student for too long. As with the clipboard cruising example in chapter 6, good teachers will devise means to move around to all students to assess what they are learning.

Good teachers will develop and use a variety of assessment strategies that provide them with information regarding instruction. Assessment will tell teachers what students know before instruction begins and whether or not students are understanding the lesson while it is being delivered, as well as what, if anything, students have learned from the lesson. The information from assessments is what drives a teacher's numerous adjustments to teaching and learning activities. As the data-driven instructional model matures, teachers will begin to make assessment of student learning a major component of teaching and learning and an ongoing process as students proceed through the curriculum.

Table 7.1 outlines questions schools can use to nurture this kind of thinking and growth in teachers. It works for collegial coaching, where two teachers are paired and observe each other's classes; for new teacher mentor programs, where a new teacher is paired with a veteran teacher in the same grade level or subject area; or for a formal teacher observation process, which includes a preconference, an observation, and a summative conference.

In any of these situations, a collegial coach, mentor, or evaluator discusses the topics with the teacher prior to the lesson. (See collegial coaching, mentoring new teachers, and teacher evaluation in the Key Resources section.)

Table 7.1.   Preconference Form

The topics outlined on the preconference form are an excellent discussion guide to encourage teachers to become more reflective about curriculum, instruction, and assessment. The preconference may be part of the teacher evaluation process or included as a component of collegial coaching or new teacher mentoring.

Teacher:	Grade/subject:		Date:
Observation Number:	Time:	Room:	Observer:

1. LEARNING CONTEXT (Relationship to unit, area of study, program goals)

2. LEARNER CHARACTERISTICS (What students are like; students with special needs or characteristics)

3. LEARNER OBJECTIVES
   CONTENT (What is to be learned?)   PROCESS (What will students be doing?)

4. ASSESSMENT
   PRE (Processes used to determine   POST (Process used to evaluate student
   level of student readiness)   learning)

5. INSTRUCTIONAL STRATEGIES AND MATERIALS (Resources, methods, techniques of teaching)

6. OBSERVER FOCUS (Major focus of data collection)

Source: From *Classroom Supervision and Instructional Improvement,* by Jerry Bellon and Elner Bellon (Dubuque: Kendall/Hunt, 1982), 36. Copyright 1982 by Kendall/Hunt Publishing Company. Reprinted with permission.

QUESTIONS TO NURTURE EFFECTIVE STANDARDS-BASED INSTRUCTION

The learner context asks the teacher how the lesson fits into the broader curriculum. Is the lesson at the beginning of a unit or the end? Does the unit focus on a state standard that is taught in a specific unit or is it a standard that is learned throughout the year? Responses to questions like these will help the teacher relate an individual lesson to the entire local curriculum and to the state standards.

Learner characteristics asks the teacher about the students. Are students progressing through the curriculum at the appropriate pace? Are there many students who require reteaching? How many students are receiving help outside of class? Instructional resource center, special education resource, other? Teachers who know their students well are more effective in helping them learn. Answers to these questions will help the teacher focus on the needs of underperforming students and groups of students.

Learner objectives includes content and process. *Content* asks the teacher, What is to be learned? This is a key question where the individual lesson is tied to the curriculum. It's asking the teacher, What do you want students to know and be able to do as a result of this lesson? This question will encourage the teacher to develop specific, measurable learner objectives rather than global, unmeasurable generalities. The English teacher whose content objective is to have students "love Shakespeare" needs help to be more specific. Students need to understand the plot, characters, and theme of *Romeo and Juliet* before they can learn to appreciate, much less love, Shakespeare. *Process* asks the teacher, What will students be doing? The answer to this question describes the activities students will be engaged in to understand the content in real and meaningful ways. There are some lessons, such as science labs or social studies problem solving activities, where process objectives should be emphasized as much as content objectives.

Assessment includes preassessment and postassessment. *Preassessment* asks the teacher to describe the processes that were used to determine student readiness. This question keeps teachers from marching through the curriculum when students are not ready to proceed because they do not know the prerequisite material. Preassessment includes the results of the last test, homework, or written assignment. Hopefully, these results will indicate that students understand the prerequisite material and are ready to proceed to the next level. *Postassessment* asks teachers how they will evaluate student learning of this lesson: How will you know if they know it? The answer may include the common local assessment, as well as the next graded homework assignment, class discussion, or rubric-graded performance.

Instructional strategies and materials asks the teacher to describe the methods and materials students will be using. Will students be in a lab setting, working in groups, listening to direct instruction, and so on.

Observer focus is the method in which the observer, be it a teacher coach, mentor, or supervisor, collects data about the lesson. A log of teacher or student verbal data or a teacher's physical movement about a classroom or lab are some of the options available to the observer.

While a standards-based curriculum, instruction, and assessment model is a useful tool to increase student achievement and meet the demands of NCLB, it only is a means to help teachers focus their instruction and help school communities decide what students should know and be able to do. The purpose of assessment, on any level, is to help teachers with the decision-making process that is ongoing in effective instruction and to answer the question, What have students learned? State standards and yearly state testing may work to improve the achievement levels of students across the country, but only if they are embraced by caring, well-trained teachers who actively engage students in a challenging, common local curriculum and thoughtful common local assessments.

KEY RESOURCES

Teaching to the Test

For a thorough discussion of the pros, cons, and legal implications of "teaching to the test," see Kober 2002.

Collegial Coaching

Collegial coaching is an effective means by which schools can increase teachers' knowledge of research-based instruction and promote reflection and analysis regarding standards-based curriculum, instruction, and assessment practices.

Collegial coaching programs generally pair two teachers in either the same or different subject areas and grade levels who are interested in working together to improve their teaching. Teachers are asked to select an area of research on which they would like to concentrate, study the research, and then implement it their classroom. Each teacher observes the other and engages in a preconference, observation, and postobservation conference. Table 7.1 serves as the basis for the preconference questions. During the observation, the observer collects data regarding teacher and/or student behavior and/or verbal statements and then using these data, reconstructs the lesson during the postobservation conference. At this time, teachers have the opportunity to reflect on the research and its effect during classroom implementation.

Teaching from a Research Knowledge Base (Bellon, Bellon, and Blank 1992) provides an excellent research review of effective instructional strategies for teachers to use and then evaluate with their collegial coaching partner.

Mentoring New Teachers

Mentor teacher programs pair a new or new-to-the-school teacher with a veteran teacher who meets the criteria for being a mentor. These criteria include being a skillful teacher, having a thorough knowledge of the curriculum being taught, understanding and practicing school rules and policies, and having the ability to transmit effective teaching practices.

The mentor introduces the new teacher to school routines and procedures, demonstrates lessons, observes the new teacher, and provides feedback. Importantly, the mentor can help a new teacher interpret a standards-based curriculum and assessment program, understand the responsibilities of team membership, and develop the skills and attitudes necessary for using test data to increase student learning and achievement. For additional information on new teacher mentor programs, see Heller and Sindelar 1991.

Teacher Evaluation

For a complete discussion of teacher evaluation using the preconference questions discussed in chapter 7 as well as an observation process and postconference format, see Bellon and Bellon 1982.

References

Bellon, J., and Bellon, E. 1982. *Classroom Supervision and Instructional Improvement.* 2nd ed. Dubuque, IA: Kendall/Hunt.

Bellon, J., Bellon, E., and Blank, M. A. 1992. *Teaching from a Research Knowledge Base.* New York: Merrill.

Bullard, P., and Taylor, B. 1993. *Making Reform Happen.* New York: Allyn & Bacon.

Chudowsky, V., and Chudowsky, N. 2004. *Rule Changes Could Help More Schools Meet Test Score Targets for the No Child Left Behind Act.* www.cep-dc.org. Accessed March 2005.

Commercial Club of Chicago. 2003. *Left Behind.* Chicago: Education Committee.

Debra P. v. Turlington, 644 F.2d. 397 U.S. Ct. App. 1981.

Dell'Angela, T. 2004. "City's Schools Get Gold Star." *Chicago Tribune,* August 5, 1.

Dufour, R., Dufour, R., Eaker, R., and Karhanek, G. 2004. *Whatever It Takes: How Professional Communities Respond When Kids Don't Learn.* Bloomington, IN: National Education Service.

Fullan, M. 2001. *Leading in a Culture of Change.* San Francisco: Jossey-Bass.

Glickman, C. 1993. *Renewing America's Schools.* San Francisco: Jossey-Bass.

Graham, M. 1998. *Teacher Developed Rubric.* Villa Park, IL: DuPage High School District 88.

Heller, M., and Sindelar, N. 1991. *Developing an Effective Mentor Teacher Program.* Bloomington, IN: Phi Delta Kappa.

Illinois State Board of Education. 1997a. *Illinois Learning Standards.* Goal 11. Springfield: Illinois State Board of Education.

———. 1997b. *Illinois Learning Standards.* Goal 15. Springfield: Illinois State Board of Education.

———. 2003a. *PSAE Social Science.* www.isbe.net/assessment/PDF/ PSAE2003data.pdf. Accessed March 2005.

———. 2003b. *2003 Statewide Performance Levels.* www.isbe.net/assessment/ PDF/PSAE2003data.pdf. Accessed March 2005.

———. 2003c. *Student Friendly Rubric for Middle/Junior High: Persuasive Expository.* www.isbe.net/assessment/MJHRubricPE.htm. Accessed March 2005.

Jennings, J., Rentner, D. S., and Kober, N. 2002. *A New Federal Role in Education.* Washington, DC: Center on Education Policy.

Kober, N. 2002. "Teaching to the Test." *TestTalk* 1. Washington, DC: Center on Education Policy.

Nevada Department of Education. 2005. *Nevada Writing Assessment Holistic Rubric.* www.doe.nv.gov/sca/standards/writing/Holistic%20rubric .html. Accessed March 2005.

Northern Illinois University. 2004. *Academic Improvement.* www.p20.niu .edu?acadimproveawards/acad_improv.shtml. Accessed July 2004.

Pinkerton, E., Kober, N., Scott, C., and Buell, B. 2003. *Implementing the No Child Left Behind Act.* Washington, DC: Center on Education Policy.

Region 10 Educational Service Center, Texas. 2000. *TAAS Mathematics.* www.ednet10.net/taas/s00/go7/i0l/q.html. Accessed March 2004.

Rosenholtz, S. 1991. *Teacher's Workplace: The Social Organization of Schools.* New York: Teachers College Press.

Stiggins, R. 2002. "Assessment for Learning." *Education Week*, March 13, 30.

U.S. Department of Education. 2002a. *The No Child Left Behind: Executive Summary.* www.ed.gov/offices/OESE/esea/exec-summ.html. Accessed February 2003.

———. 2002b. *The No Child Left Behind: Fact Sheet.* www.ed.gov/offices/ OESE/esea/factsheet.html. Accessed February 2003.

Wiggins, G. 1993. *Assessing Student Performance.* San Francisco: Jossey-Bass.

Index

About the Author

Nancy W. Sindelar, Ph.D., writes on educational topics and is a consultant to schools in the areas of curriculum and assessment; collection, use, and interpretation of student test data; teacher mentorship; and staff evaluation. Dr. Sindelar brings to these endeavors over thirty years' experience in public education as a teacher, department chair, assistant principal, and assistant superintendent for curriculum, instruction, and assessment. She also has taught graduate courses in school supervision, school law, and educational assessment and has spoken at numerous national conferences, including meetings of the Association for Supervision and Curriculum Development, American Association of School Administrators, and the National Association of School Boards.

Dr. Sindelar received her bachelor's degree from Northwestern University, a master's degree from DePaul University, a certificate of advanced studies from Concordia University, and a doctor of philosophy degree from Loyola University of Chicago. She was a visiting scholar with the English faculty at Cambridge University and served a four-year term as president of Northwestern University's School of Education and Social Policy Alumni Board. She can be reached at Sindelar37@aol.com.